7 CRUCIAL QUESTIONS About the BIBLE

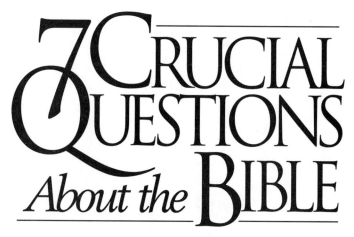

7 CRUCIAL QUESTIONS About the BIBLE

(And How the Answers Will Strengthen Your Faith)

JAMES C. DENISON

BROADMAN
&HOLMAN
PUBLISHERS

Nashville, Tennessee

4211-62
0-8054-1162-3

Dewey Decimal Classification: 220.07
Subject Heading: BIBLE—STUDY
Library of Congress Card Catalog Number: 93-40466
Printed in the United States of America

Scripture quotations marked (KJV) are from the King James Version of the Bible; (NIV) the Holy Bible, New International Version, © 1973, 1978, 1984 by International Bible Society; (REB), the Revised English Bible, © Oxford University Press and Cambridge University Press, 1989, reprinted by permission; (RSV) the Revised Standard Version of the Bible, © 1946, 1952, 1971, 1973; and (TLB)The Living Bible, Paraphrased, © Tyndale House Publishers, Wheaton, Ill., 1971, used by permission.

Library of Congress Cataloging-in-Publication Data
Denison, James C., 1958–
    7 crucial questions about the Bible and how the answers will strengthen your faith.
        p. cm.
    ISBN 0-8054-1162-3
    1. Bible—Study and teaching.   I. Title.
    BS600.2.D385   1994
    220'.07—dc20   93-40466
                                                                    CIP

CONTENTS

WHY THIS BOOK?

It was he who gave some to be apostles, some to be prophets, some to
be evangelists, and some to be pastors and teachers, to prepare God's
people for works of service.
— (Ephesians 4:11–12)

These words are my "life text." They are the reason I go to
work at my church every day. I believe that God has called
me to "prepare God's people for works of service." I would
like to tell you why and how this book resulted from that call.

I grew up in Houston, Texas. My parents raised my younger
brother and me to be good, moral people, to live honestly and to work
hard. Although we did not attend church a great deal, we grew up
believing in God and the Bible. The problem was, I had never
bothered to learn what the Bible actually says, or who God really is.

It was a steamy Saturday morning in August of 1973 when all that
began to change. The Baptist church in our neighborhood had just
begun a "bus ministry"—men would knock on doors on Saturday
mornings, searching for youth and children to ride their bus to
church on Sunday. That morning, Julian Unger and Tony McGrady
knocked on my door. I didn't want to go, but Dad encouraged us.

After that first Sunday, riding on the bus became a fairly regular pattern. The bus ministry men continued to visit. The church continued to pray for us. The other teenagers in the church showed me God's love through their love. Finally I asked my Sunday School teacher how I could have the joy they had, and she led me to personal faith in Jesus Christ as Savior and Lord. Six months later my brother came to Christ, and a year later we were baptized together. Today Mark is pastor of a church he started in Houston several years ago.

My point is this: I came to Christ because people in the church first came to me. Julian Unger and Tony McGrady were God's first ministers in my life. Were it not for their witness, I probably would be without Christ today. God used His people to bring Christ to me, knowing I would never have come to Him myself.

I believe that most unchurched people are like I was. They will probably not come to our churches to hear preachers like me today. Our people must go to them where they work, go to school, and live. God's people must do "works of service."

This was always Jesus' plan for evangelizing the world. If I could bring one person to Christ a day for the rest of my active ministry, I would help over four thousand people experience God's love. This is evangelism by addition—I work to add people to God's kingdom. I'm grateful for any way someone comes to God, but evangelism by addition was never God's plan. He wants us to grow by multiplication.

Here's how His plan works. I would bring someone today to Jesus, and teach him how to share his faith so that he could help someone else come to Christ. Then tomorrow, he wins someone while I win someone. We teach them to share their faith, and the next day they win others while we win others. This is evangelism by multiplication.

Do you know how long this plan would take to win our entire world to Christ? Winning and discipling one person per day, we could reach the entire population of our planet *in thirty-one days!* You may not believe it, as I didn't at first. Try it at a calculator. You'll find that it's true.

Here's the catch: we have to teach those we bring to Christ how to bring others to Him. We must "prepare God's people for works of service." Those who are called to lead the church—the apostles, prophets, evangelists, and pastors and teachers—must equip the church to do its ministry. As the saying goes, "shepherds don't make sheep—sheep make sheep."

And so I have devoted my life to helping God's people learn how to do their ministries. After teaching on the faculty of Southwestern Baptist Theological Seminary, God called me to bring this teaching ministry to First Baptist Church in Midland, Texas.

My heart's desire is to teach Christians how to be the ministers God has called them to be. As a result, in Midland our church has begun a "lay seminary" to teach our people ministry knowledge and skills. We call it "Growing in Grace: The Equipping Ministry of First Baptist Church." Courses are offered for our people in a variety of ministry topics. Since we started this approach, we've seen God use the courses to change lives and equip ministers. It's been one of the most exciting works of which I've ever been part.

That's where this book enters the picture. God's basic tool for training His people to minister is the Bible. Learning about His Word and how to study it is our first step in His plan for equipping His people. For this reason, we began our equipping ministry with the class, How to Understand the Bible.

In the course we touched on subjects about the Bible which are unfamiliar to most laypeople. In essence, I tried to answer their questions about God's word. Because of the popularity and apparent effectiveness of the course, I wanted to share these questions and answers with a broader audience. This book is the result.

Three words about the format:

First, the questions are arranged in a logical order, so that the answers can build on previous studies. Second, several "Check Yourself " sections are included in each chapter, so that you can better remember key facts and information. The answers are at the end of the chapters. I hope you will use the book as a kind of classroom experience. Third, endnotes are included, for two reasons. First, it is important that you be familiar with the best academic sources. The results of scholarship need to be made available to our people today. Second, I want to point you to resources for additional study on your own. The endnotes may help you in this area.

My goal for 7 *Crucial Questions About the Bible* is very simple: to help God's people better understand His Word, so that they can do their ministries more effectively. If these pages help to "prepare God's people for works of service," I will be most grateful.

1

WHY DO WE READ THE BIBLE?

The Importance of God's Word

My earliest memory of the Bible is of an old, tattered, black book, sitting high up on a shelf. It was out of reach, dusty, old, unused. That's what I thought the Bible was. I was wrong.

In 1991 a record 83 million-plus Bibles, New Testaments, and Scripture portions were distributed throughout the world. This was a 16 percent increase over the record-breaking figures of the year before.[1] Contrary to my childhood opinion, the Bible is a popular book.

The Bible is also a powerful book. George Washington said, "It is impossible to righteously govern the world without God and the Bible." Andrew Jackson called the Bible "the rock on which our republic rests." In a recent poll, 223 corporate CEOs and college presidents named the Bible as the most influential book in their lives.[2]

And the Bible is a controversial book as well. Consider the situation faced by the Gideons in Indiana. That state owns and operates six inns in its state parks. The Gideons place a Bible in each room of these hotels. Recently, however, the state's Department of Natural Resources was forced to place warning pamphlets in the rooms as well. These pamphlets include a picture of the Bible with these words stamped across it: "Warning! Literal belief in this book may endanger your life and health." The American Civil Liberties Union had threatened a lawsuit if these pamphlets were not used.[3]

So, what is the Bible? This is the single most important question we should ask in unlocking God's word. You see, nearly all the problems people have in understanding the Bible start with misunderstandings of what the book *is*. Only when you know what the Bible is and why it was written can you understand its message for your life.

This is true of most things in life—they work best when they're used according to their purpose. A power saw doesn't make a good screwdriver or a blender a good oven. No one would play tennis with a football or sew with a hammer. Neither should we study and apply the Bible until we know its purpose. And so, listen to Mortimer Adler's now-famous warning about all books: "Rule 1. You must know what kind of book you are reading, and you should know this as early in the process as possible, preferably before you begin to read."[4] He was especially right about the Bible. We need to know what the Bible *is* before we can know what it *means*. So, what is the Bible, and why is it so important that we read it? And what principles for Bible study can we discover in answering these questions?

God's Book

Prophecy never had its origin in the will of man, but men spoke from God as they were carried along by the Holy Spirit. (2 Peter 1:21)

First and foremost, the Bible is God's book. It is important that we read this book, because the God of the universe wrote it. He used men to compose its words, but these men were "carried along" by His Spirit. God created the Bible, for us.

This fact leads us to our first guiding principle for Bible study: *You can understand God's word, for this is the intent of its Author.* This principle is very important. God gave you His word, and He wants to help you understand it. He did not write to hide Himself but to reveal Himself to you. He wants you to understand His book.

To help make this point, let's look at the three most popular names for the Bible today. Each of them underscores the fact that the Bible is important as God's book for us.

THE HOLY BIBLE

We usually call God's book the "Holy Bible." We should, because "God's book" is what "Holy Bible" literally means.

The word "bible" comes from Byblos, an ancient town in Phoenicia east of the Mediterranean Sea. This town gave its name to the plant whose leaves were used to make the paper of the day. Out of these "byblos" leaves books were produced. Incidentally, this plant was known to the Egyptians as "papyrus," from which we get our word "paper." The word "bible," then, literally means "book."

"Holy" means "set apart," "sacred," or "divine." This word applies most fully to God, the "Holy One." Putting the two terms together, the "Holy Bible" means "God's book." The Holy Bible is literally the "book of God."⁵

THE SCRIPTURES

Second, we often refer to the Bible as the "Scriptures." This word means "writings." "Scripture" is a title which the Bible sometimes uses for itself (for example, Acts 18:28; 2 Tim. 3:16; and 2 Pet. 3:16). The Bible is God's "writings" to us. It is His book.

An important note: All the Bible is God's Scripture. For instance, Paul used the word "Scripture" for books found today in both the Old and the New Testaments when he wrote, "For the Scripture says, 'Do not muzzle the ox while it is treading out the grain,' and 'The worker deserves his wages'" (1 Tim. 5:18). Paul's first reference comes from Deuteronomy 25:4, and his second is from Jesus' words in Luke 10:7. Paul considered both the Old and the New "writings" to be divine "Scripture." Peter also used the word "Scripture" in referring to Paul's letters (see 2 Pet. 3:16). All of the Bible is God's "Scripture" to us.

THE WORD OF GOD

Third, the Bible is often called the "word of God," God's very words. In fact, the Bible often uses this term for itself (for example, Matt. 15:6; John 10:35; and Heb. 4:12). This book is "God's book" because it gives the very words of God to us today.

The Bible is God's book, His writings, His word to us. He went to great, even miraculous lengths to give us this book. Obviously He wants us to understand what He has given. It's an astounding fact—the Creator of the universe and Lord of eternity has written a book, and He wants you to understand it!

CHECK YOURSELF I

1. The word "bible" literally means _____.

2. "Holy" literally means _____ _____.

3. "Scripture" literally means _____.

4. T/F: The Bible is intended to be difficult to study and understand.

5. T/F: Paul seems to indicate that he considers only the Old Testament to be God's "scripture."

A REVEALING BOOK

The Word of God is living and active. Sharper than any double-edged sword, it penetrates even to dividing soul and spirit, joints and marrow; it judges the thoughts and attitudes of the heart. (Hebrews 4:12)

Why does God want you to understand His book? It is because He wants you to know Him. The Bible is an important book, for here God reveals Himself to you.

People have often had trouble believing that God would reveal Himself to us. Euripides (480–406 B.C.), the Greek playwright, was pessimistic about knowing God:

Past our telling, the ways of heaven. The gods accomplish the unforeseen. What all awaited, fails of achievement; God arranges what none could dream.[6]

Many today are just as pessimistic. I know people who call themselves "agnostics." These are persons who claim that we *cannot* know God. He may exist, but we can never know Him personally.

The facts are otherwise. God *has* revealed Himself to us, in His world and in His word. This means that we can know about Him and know Him personally. Now, how has He done this?

How God Reveals Himself

The World. You can tell a great deal about someone if you examine his or her work. An artist reveals her personality and perspective on life in her art. A musician shows his mood and character in the way he performs. A factory worker reveals his integrity in the quality of what he makes. The work reveals the worker.

This is also true of God and His world—the Creator reveals Himself in His creation. The Psalmist sings, "The heavens declare the glory of God; the skies proclaim the work of His hands" (Ps. 19:1). In our world we have evidence enough to believe that God is a purposeful, powerful, glorious Creator (see Acts 14:17).

However, there's a problem. When Adam and Eve sinned by breaking God's direct command, God's creation was tainted by sin and no longer reveals Him perfectly (see Rom. 8:22). Even more important, the fall also corrupted our minds with sin so that we are unable to find God fully in His creation (see Rom. 1:18–23). God revealed Himself in His world, but we can no longer know enough of Him on that basis to have personal relationship with Him.

The Word. For this reason God revealed Himself to us not only by the world but also by the word. For ancient people, this would be equally as powerful a revelation. God's words are creative: "By the word of the Lord were the heavens made, their starry host by the breath of His mouth" (Ps. 33:6). His words are powerful, always accomplishing His purpose for them (Isa. 55:10–11). And words are revelatory, binding the one who utters them and revealing his character (see Gen. 27:32–38). For these reasons God has used the "word" to reveal Himself to us. There are three ways He has done so.

First, He shows Himself to us in His Son, the "Word" of God. Writing about Jesus, John declares, "In the beginning was the Word, and the Word was with God, and the Word was God" (John 1:1). Jesus is the "Word" of God because He is God's own statement about Himself to us. What the Father is, He has shown to us in His Son. God reveals Himself through His "incarnate" ("made flesh") Word, Jesus Christ.

Second, God reveals Himself in His written word, the Bible. The Bible tells us about God's Son, intending to draw us to Him in faith.

Third, God uses our words today. When we teach His written word and tell about His Son, we reveal God to others. This brings up an important point, however: God's Son and Scriptures always take precedence over our words. We are not inspired as was the Bible. Nor do we possess the authority of Jesus. We must always judge our words by Jesus and the Scriptures. But when we preach Christ and teach the Bible properly, God uses our words to reveal Himself to others (see 1 Cor. 1:21).

Before we leave this section, notice something very important: The Bible is at the center of God's revelation. Without the Bible we would know very little about Jesus. And without the Bible we would have very little to preach and teach. The Bible is God's chief means of revealing Himself to us today.

How We Meet God in the Bible

If God gave us His word to reveal Himself to us, this raises a second question: How do we meet Him there? How does Bible study lead us to experience God? The answer: God's word reveals to us our need for God, and then shows how He meets this need in Christ. The Bible is an important, revealing book because it shows us how God meets our deepest needs today.

The Bible reveals our need for God. When we read the Bible, we come face to face with our sin problem and need for God. This is why Dwight Moody, the famous evangelist of the nineteenth century, wrote in a Bible he gave to a friend, "This book will separate you from your sins, or your sins will separate you from this book." The Bible reveals our sin problem.

The Bible shows us that we all have this problem: "All have sinned and fall short of the glory of God" (Rom. 3:23). It shows us the result of this sin: "The wages of sin is death" (Rom. 6:23). The Bible reveals the proper punishment of all who sin: "Depart from me, you who are cursed, into the eternal fire prepared for the devil and his angels" (Matt. 25:41). And God's word reveals the future for all who reject Christ and are therefore removed from God's "book of life": "If anyone's name was not found written in the book of life, he was thrown into the lake of fire" (Rev. 20:15). Moody was right—the Bible was written to separate you from your sins.

The Bible reveals God's answer to our need. Once God has shown us our problem, He reveals Jesus as the only solution. The Bible says that God's Son is our only hope: "Christ in you, the hope of glory" (Col. 1:27). God's word reveals Christ as our salvation: "God so loved the world that He gave His one and only Son, that whoever believes in Him shall not perish but have eternal life" (John 3:16). It states that Christ is the only way to God: "Jesus answered, 'I am the way and the truth and the life. No one comes to the Father except through me'" (John 14:6). And the Bible promises that Jesus is our way to triumphant living: "I have come that they may have life, and have it to the full" (John 10:10).

In the Bible God shows you your sin and its devastation, and then He shows you His solution in Christ. God wants you to respond to this revelation by turning to Christ as Savior and Lord. When you do this, in Christ you experience God. The Bible leads you to a personal relationship with the Lord.

This is true of any problem you have. When you study the Bible for God's answer to your need and you obey what He reveals to you, you experience Him personally. You have not only His answer to your problem, but also His personal help in His Spirit. The Bible becomes your bridge to relationship with its Author.

Here we find our second guiding principle for Bible study: The purpose of Bible study is to experience God. John made this clear: the Scriptures were written "that you may believe that Jesus is the Christ, the Son of God, and that by believing you may have life in His name" (John 20:31). Whenever you study the Bible, you have the opportunity to come into the presence of its Author. As God reveals your need and His answer, you trust in Him. And your faith draws you personally to God.

In discussing the importance of the Bible, we've discovered two guiding principles for Bible study: (1) God wants you to understand

His book. The Bible is a clear Word which you can study for yourself.
(2) The Scriptures exist to reveal their Author so that you can know
and experience Him personally. Our goal for all Bible study is nothing
short of this: to meet and understand God.

CHECK YOURSELF 2

1. T/F: Because of sin, we can no longer know enough of God
    on the basis of His creation to have a personal relationship with
    Him.

2. How has God used the "Word" to reveal Himself to us?

    a. _____

    b. _____

    c. _____

3. T/F: God's written word stands under the authority of our
    interpretation today.

4. The _____ is God's chief means of revealing Himself
    to us today: (choose one)

    a. church

    b. preached word

    c. Bible

    d. world

5. The primary purpose of Bible study is: (choose one)

    a. to learn more about God's word

    b. to experience God

    c. to become a better Bible teacher

    d. to win theological debates with your friends

An Inspired Book

All Scripture is God-breathed and is useful for teaching, rebuking, correcting and training in righteousness, so that the man of God may be thoroughly equipped for every good work. (2 Timothy 3:16–17)

So far we've answered two questions about the Bible: what is it? and why was it written? We've discovered that the Bible by *nature* is God's word. God gave it to us to be understood. And we've seen that the Bible by *purpose* was written to help us know Him personally. Now let's think about a third, very important subject: what is the Bible's origin? The answer is: by God's "inspiration."

Inspiration means more than that the Bible is "inspiring." Most people agree that the Bible is indeed an inspiring book, one of the greatest literary achievements of all time. But it is much more: it is not only inspiring but also inspired.[7]

The word "inspire" means "to breathe into." When we use this word about the Bible, we mean that God "breathed" His words to us. As Paul says in the passage above, the Bible is "God-breathed" to us. These are God's own words for us today.

This brings us to a third guiding principle for Bible study: you should approach the Bible as the very word of God. You can trust this book without hesitation. And you should study it with deep and humble reverence. The inspiration of the Bible means that the Bible is God's word for you.

But there's more to the story. There were two sides to the process of making the Bible: the divine and the human. God "breathed out" the Bible, but He used men to record His word. The more you know about both sides of the Bible—the divine and the human—the more you can appreciate both its authority from God and its importance for us.

The Bible's Divine Side

What the Bible Says. The Bible clearly and consistently claims God for its Author. Jeremiah, like all the Old Testament prophets, credited the origin of his words to God. He wrote, "The Word of the Lord came to me, saying" (Jer. 1:4). Peter, referring to the Old Testament, said, "Prophecy never had its origin in the will of man, but men spoke from God as they were carried along by the Holy Spirit" (2 Pet. 1:21).

And Jesus gave us a divine endorsement of the Old Testament when He predicted: "I tell you the truth, until heaven and earth disappear, not the smallest letter, not the least stroke of a pen, will by any means disappear from the Law until everything is accomplished" (Matt. 5:18).

The New Testament writers were also conscious of God's hand on their work. For example, Paul says of his words, "The gospel I preached is not something that man made up. I did not receive it from any man, nor was I taught it; rather, I received it by revelation from Jesus Christ" (Gal. 1:11–12). He made the same statement to the Corinthians: "This is what we speak, not in words taught us by human wisdom but in words taught by the Spirit" (1 Cor. 2:13). What's more, his statement that all Scripture is "inspired" by God (2 Tim. 3:16) clearly names God as the source of all the Bible. The Bible clearly claims divine authorship for itself.

Support for the Biblical Claims. We have a problem, however. Just because a book claims to be from God doesn't necessarily make it so. You see, other religions make the same claim for their writings. Muslims believe their holy book, the "Koran," was dictated in Arabic to Muhammad by Allah ("God"). Latter-day Saints believe that Joseph Smith discovered the Book of Mormon ready-made on golden plates which only he could translate. Many Eastern religions teach that their masters' words were given by direct inspiration of their god or gods. What evidence besides the Bible do we have that the Bible is God's word?[8]

A thorough study of this subject would fill an entire book. We can, however, sketch briefly four answers to this question. First, there are the early copies of the Bible, known as the "manuscripts." While we don't possess the actual documents which the biblical authors wrote, our earliest copies of them are excellent, numerous, and come very close in age to the originals. This is more true for the Bible than for any other ancient book in existence today, including the other religious books mentioned above. Scholars call this kind of comparison the "bibliographic" test. (For more on this subject, see pp. 33–36 below.) We can trust our Bible today to be God's word because it is based on excellent ancient copies of the original documents themselves.

Second, there is the evidence of archaeology. This science seeks to recover and interpret the remains and records of ancient civilizations.

Archaeologists often make discoveries which validate the historical records of the Bible. In 1993 an Israeli archaeologist uncovered an inscription near the Syrian border that refers to the House of David. This is the first evidence outside the Bible that David founded a dynasty that ruled ancient Israel. Biblical scholars called the find "sensational."[9] And so, we can trust the Bible to be God's word because archaeology verifies its records.

Third, there is fulfilled prophecy. Bible predictions have come to pass in hundreds of ways. Consider these predictions regarding the coming of Jesus: He was to be born in Bethlehem (Micah 5:2); He would minister in Galilee (Isa. 9:1–2); He would be rejected by the Jews (Isa. 53:3); He would enter triumphantly into Jerusalem (Zech. 9:9); He would suffer crucifixion (Isa. 53:4–7,12); He would be raised from the dead (Ps. 16:10). Of course, Jesus fulfilled each of these predictions. On this subject and many others, biblical prophecies have been fulfilled. The Bible keeps its promises, showing that it is from God.

Fourth, there is personal experience. The Bible claims that in its pages you can meet God. Millions of Christians across twenty centuries can verify that this claim is true. As you experience God in the Bible, you give personal proof of its divine origin.

THE BIBLE'S HUMAN SIDE

While the Bible is divine in its origin, that's only half of the story. God "breathed" His word to us, but He did this through men. He did not shout the Bible in an audible voice from the sky or write it on heavenly paper and drop it to earth. He spoke both to us and through us in creating His word.

How did God use men in writing His word? Once He literally wrote His word for them. In creating the Ten Commandments and their related laws, "When the Lord finished speaking to Moses on Mount Sinai, he gave Him the two tablets of the Testimony, the tablets of stone inscribed by the finger of God" (Ex. 31:18).

There were times when God spoke in an audible voice to men and women. "When the Lord saw that [Moses] had gone over to look, God called to him from within the bush, 'Moses! Moses!' And Moses said, 'Here I am'" (Ex. 3:4).

Sometimes God spoke through dreams. Joseph had this experience: "An angel of the Lord appeared to Him in a dream and said, 'Joseph son of David, do not be afraid to take Mary home as your wife'" (Matt. 1:20). God spoke audibly through His angels as well, as in announcing the birth of Christ to the shepherds (Luke 2:8–14). The Lord indeed worked "at sundry times and in divers manners" to get His word to us (Heb. 1:1, KJV).

Most often, however, the Lord used the minds and personalities of the biblical authors as His way of bringing His word to us. It's important to know that these authors vary in their writing styles and goals. Many of the biblical writers were historians and all of them were theologians and authors in their own right.[10]

Historians. Genesis tells of the beginnings of world history and the origin of the people of Israel. Exodus and Numbers describe the people's escape from Egypt and their wilderness wanderings. Joshua details the Hebrews' conquest of the Promised Land. The books of Kings and Chronicles tell the stories of the Hebrew kings. And Ezra and Nehemiah describe the exile and return of the people from Babylon. The gospels tell the story of Jesus' earthly ministry, while Acts describes the history and growth of the first church. Nearly half of the Bible is devoted to history.

Some of this history was obviously given directly by God. How could a human author know the story of the beginnings of the universe apart from God's direct disclosure? Often, however, the authors also used historical research in their writings. Luke says that he "carefully investigated" the records of the eyewitnesses to the life of Christ when he wrote his gospel (see Luke 1:1–4). It seems clear, therefore, that divine and human authorship are not incompatible. God could and did use human minds and research in giving His word to us.

Theologians. The biblical historians were not historians in the modern sense. They made no attempt to achieve the kind of scientific detachment historians often claim today. Rather, all of the biblical writers were theologians, writing from the perspective of faith. Their goal was to tell about God, to tell "His Story" through their writings. As a result the Old Testament historical books show God as the hero and creator of the events they describe, and the gospels were written by evangelists who wanted their readers to trust in Jesus.

This explains the different perspectives from which the biblical books were written. Paul, the Pharisee set free, writes of grace; Luke, the Gentile, stresses the universal appeal of the gospel; and John, the pastor, tells of the love of Jesus. God used the background and goals of each biblical author to give a part of His word to us.

Authors. The biblical writers were each authors in their own right. They used their own vocabularies and writing styles and wrote their books to make the greatest literary impact on their readers. Amos' preaching of judgment reads quite differently from Hosea's pleas of love. Matthew's gospel, written for Jews, specifically cites Old Testament prophets sixteen times; Luke, writing for Gentiles, makes almost no reference to the Old Testament. Luke, highly educated in the technical Greek of first-century scholars, writes in a complex style, while Mark uses short, concrete sentences.

We can see, then, that just as the Bible claims God for its author, it also reveals that men were the means by which He did His work. If we are to be fair to this book we are seeking to understand, we must hold its divine and human sides together without either overriding the other. While God indeed "breathed out" His very word to us, He chose not to obliterate but to use the minds of the men who wrote that word. At the same time, the men who wrote from their individual perspectives never distorted the message of the Author.

How the Divine and the Human Relate

How *did* God use men to get His word to us? Scholars call this "the question of inspiration." This is a difficult and sometimes controversial subject. Nevertheless, we must study it briefly in order to know how to keep both aspects of the Bible together.

First, let's dispense with three popular but mistaken theories. Many today believe the Bible is "inspired" like all great literature—no more and no less. Scholars refer to this as the "natural" inspiration theory. Others argue that the Bible was only inspired to the same degree as Christian writing and preaching today. This is called the "general Christian" theory. Still others accept as inspired only certain sections of the Bible. This is called the "partial inspiration" theory. The Bible itself rejects each of these theories by claiming God's special authorship of all the Scriptures (2 Tim. 3:16).

Now let's look at three theories which deserve our attention. These are the most popular among Bible-believing Christians today, and each provides some help in understanding inspiration better.

Dictation. The "dictation" theory teaches that God gave each of the literal words of the Bible directly to their human writers. In this view, the biblical authors functioned something like stenographers. As we have seen, this is clearly the way some of the Bible came to us (the Ten Commandments, for example). The problem is that it doesn't leave room for the human elements of the Bible which we discussed earlier. The biblical books do reflect their human authors' different vocabularies, writing styles, and goals. For this reason the "dictation" theory is not popular with most scholars today.

Verbal. A second approach is the "verbal" theory. Those who adopt this approach teach that God inspired the individual words of the Bible while also allowing the writers' personalities to be used. This view is usually combined with the word "plenary," meaning "all." Taken together, the "verbal plenary" view teaches that God took the initiative in inspiring each of the individual words of the Bible, but He did this in such a way as to use the writers' personalities also.

Dynamic. A third approach is called the "dynamic" theory. Those who hold this view believe that God *guided* the writers more often than He gave each word literally to them. In this way their personalities were used while God's purpose was achieved. This approach, while not insisting on the direct verbal inspiration of the individual words of the Bible, still maintains the divine inspiration of the larger text. A.H. Strong, the much-respected theologian of the early twentieth century, states the theory this way:

> The Scripture writers appear to have been so influenced by the Holy Spirit that they perceived and felt even the new truths they were to publish, as discoveries of their own minds, and were left to the action of their own minds in the expression of these truths, with the single exception that they were supernaturally held back from the selection of wrong words, and when needful were provided with right ones.[11]

This view holds that inspiration is verbal not so much in its method as in its result.

Keeping the Divine and the Human Together. Which of these theories is correct? The best answer is that all three ideas contain truths which should be combined into one concept. We should affirm *both* the divine *and* the human elements behind the creating of the Bible, without allowing either to dominate the other.

There are places in the Bible where each theory applies. Sometimes God dictated His words; at times He gave the writers His words in other direct ways; and at other times He allowed and used their free thinking. Thus the Bible is the product of *both* the divine *and* the human.

Perhaps an analogy can help clear up some confusion here. Many writers, both ancient and modern, have compared the divine/human authorship of the Bible to the divine/human nature of its subject, Jesus Christ. If we believe that Jesus could be fully divine and at the same time fully human, perhaps we can believe that the Bible is authored both by God and by men. If Jesus could be fully divine without losing His humanity, then by analogy the Bible could be fully God's word and still the work of men. If Jesus could be fully human and yet Lord, by analogy the Bible could be the work of men and yet God's authoritative word.

This analogy helps us to affirm both the divine and the human elements of the words of the Bible. We can believe that God gave us the very words of the text, so that they are absolutely reliable. At the same time we can believe that God used the personalities of the authors themselves in writing these words. As with Christ, so with His word: we must keep both the divine and the human together. Some early Christians denied Jesus' humanity and so committed heresy; others rejected Jesus' divinity and so denied the faith. We must be careful to keep both together.

Holding two truths together is essential with nearly every Christian doctrine, including the inspiration of the Bible. We teach God is three Persons and yet One. We know that the Lord directs His world, but we also know that we have a free will by which we make our own decisions. As is true with most great truths of the faith, we must "believe that we might understand." If our finite minds could completely understand the great truths of God, we might question whether these truths were truly the Lord's.

The Bible is the inspired word of God for us. God has made sure that we have the words He wants us to understand. He used men as

His means of writing this word, without allowing them to distort His truth. The Bible is God's word, and yet a word given through men. The result is important: you have a Bible which you can trust and understand. The Bible is God's word. Thus, we approach the Scriptures with deep trust and humility. The words John Calvin prayed each time he opened the Bible are appropriate for us as well:

> O Lord, heavenly Father, in whom is the fullness of light and wisdom, enlighten our minds by your Holy Spirit, and give us grace to receive your word with reverence and humility, without which no one can understand your Truth. For Christ's sake, Amen.[12]

CHECK YOURSELF 3

1. Match the term on the left with the correct definition on the right:

   ____ Inspire

   a. God guided the writers

   ____ Manuscripts

   b. Comparing the documents of ancient books

   ____ The "bibliographic" test

   c. "Breathe into"

   ____ The "dictation" theory

   d. God gave the literal words to the writers

   ____ The "verbal" theory

   e. God inspired the individual words while allowing the use of writers' personalities

   ____ The "dynamic" theory

   f. The early copies of the Bible

2. T/F: God often required the biblical authors to do historical research in their work.

3. T/F: The biblical authors give little evidence of different personalities or styles in their work.

An Authoritative Book

Heaven and earth will pass away, but my words will never pass away. (Matthew 24:35)

So far we have discovered three answers to our question, Why read the Bible? We should read it because it is God's book. It is a revealing book, intended to help us know God. It is an inspired book, given by God. From these facts we have discovered three principles for Bible study: (1) the Bible is meant to be understood, for this is the intent of its Author; (2) the purpose of Bible study is to experience God; and (3) we should approach the Bible with trust and reverence, for here we find the very Word of God.

Now, one last answer deserves our attention: the Bible is important because it is an authoritative book. Precisely because it is God's book, His revealing book, and His inspired book, the Scripture is His authoritative word for us.

From this fact we discover our last guiding principle for Bible study: *You must obey what you learn in the Bible.* The Bible only accomplishes God's purpose for it when you are obedient to the truths you learn there. You must obey the Bible as God's authority in your life.

No human words can take the place of the Bible or claim authority over it. No creeds, doctrines or other words of men or women can stand in judgment over the Scriptures.[13] The purpose of our words *about* the Bible must always be to draw people to *obey* the Bible.

Three facts can help us to understand better what the authority of the Bible means for us and for our Bible study.

The Bible Claims Authority

The Bible consistently claims authority for its truths. As God's book, it reflects His authority in its pages (2 Pet. 1:21). As God's revelation, the Bible possesses authority to reveal Christ (John 20:31). Since it was inspired by God, the Bible communicates the authoritative words of the Lord (2 Tim. 3:16).

Note, however, that the Bible's authority comes from that of its Author. While the Bible is an outstanding literary achievement on its own merits, its life-changing authority and application come not from its own words but from the Spirit who inspired them.

This is an important point, one which sets Christians apart from other religious groups. Muslims treat the Koran as inherently holy, washing their hands even before touching its pages. Many in other faiths reverence their religious books as holy or powerful in themselves. But Christians are different. Across the centuries we have always honored the Scriptures, but not worshiped them. We know that their power to transform our lives comes from the living Lord. This is why we seek the leadership of God's Spirit in studying the Bible and meeting the Lord there.

Biblical Authority Transcends Time

The Scriptures were of course authoritative for their first readers, but they are still God's authority for our lives today. This timeless authority is claimed for both the Old and the New Testaments. Notice Isaiah 40:8: "The grass withers and the flowers fall, but the word of our God stands forever." Peter applied this claim to the New Testament when he quoted Isaiah 40:8 and added, "And this is the word that was preached to you" (1 Pet. 1:25). Jesus settles the issue: "My words will never pass away" (Matt. 24:35).

The eighteenth-century French skeptic Voltaire predicted the demise of the Bible within his generation. Shortly after his death, his home was purchased by a Bible society and is still used today for the printing of the Scriptures. The authority of the Bible is truly timeless. This timeless power may be seen in the Bible's unchanging relevance. Other books will gain and lose popularity, but the Bible will always remain God's authority in our lives.

I will never forget my first experience with the oldest New Testament copies we have. They are on display at the British Museum in London in a room filled with ancient books from around the world. These two documents, called *Codex Sinaiticus* and *Codex Alexandrinus*, are two of the three earliest complete New Testaments in the world, and are the basis for much of the New Testament we study today. I stood before them in fascination for nearly an hour. During that time, not one other visitor to the museum tried to look at them. But during that same hour, hundreds of awed tourists filed past an exhibit of Beatles memorabilia some thirty feet away. I thought to myself that my children and grandchildren will not remember the Beatles, but they'll always stand under the word of God.

John Stott combines the authority and relevance of the Bible in a very insightful way:

> The modern world detests authority but worships relevance. So to bracket these two words in relation to the Bible is to claim for it one quality (authority) which people fear it has but wish it had not, and another (relevance) which they fear it has not but wish it had.

> Our Christian conviction is that the Bible has both authority and relevance—to a degree quite extraordinary in so ancient a book.[14]

This is why you must obey what you learn in the Scriptures. The Bible is still God's authority for our lives today.

BIBLICAL AUTHORITY IS LIFE-TRANSFORMING

Power is of little good unless it serves a good purpose. The purpose of biblical authority is clear: to transform your life by a personal encounter with Jesus Christ. The Scriptures are empowered by the Holy Spirit to reveal Jesus to you in a life-changing way.

What kinds of life-transformation can take place when you study the Bible? First, in the Bible the Holy Spirit judges your heart:

> The Word of God is living and active. Sharper than any double-edged sword, it penetrates even to dividing soul and spirit, joints and marrow; it judges the thoughts and attitudes of the heart. (Heb. 4:12)

Second, in the Bible the Spirit leads you to faith in Christ:

> These [things] are written that you may believe that Jesus is the Christ, the Son of God, and that by believing you may have life in His name. (John 20:31)

Third, the Bible is able by God's power to help you find security in your salvation:

> I write these things to you who believe in the name of the Son of God so that you may know that you have eternal life. (1 John 5:13)

Fourth, the Scriptures are able to equip you for Christian ministry, so that you can bring the biblical message of a secure salvation to others:

All Scripture is God-breathed and is useful for teaching, rebuking, correcting and training in righteousness, so that the man of God may be thoroughly equipped for every good work. (2 Tim. 3:16–17)

People today are more open than ever before to this life-transforming book. In 1990 at the Moscow International Book Fair, religious publishers were allowed for the first time to distribute Bibles. In earlier years they could exhibit the Scriptures but could not give Bibles to those who wanted them.

Taking advantage of this new opportunity, publishers distributed more than ten thousand copies of the New Testament in contemporary Russian. Soon the Bible exhibit became the most popular at the fair. Russians stood in long lines waiting for a book which most had never owned and many had never seen.

Nearby was the exhibit of the American Atheist Press, headed by Madelyn Murray O'Hair. Johnnie Godwin, then president of Holman Bible Publishers for The Sunday School Board of the Southern Baptist Convention, noticed that few people visited the atheist exhibit, though thousands walked by it each day. He took a now-famous picture of the scene. In the foreground hundreds of people are standing in line for Bibles, and in the background Mrs. O'Hair sits alone in her booth. The Bible continues to transform lives today.

Check Yourself 4

1. The purpose of our words about the Bible must always be to draw people to _____ the Bible.

2. T/F: The Bible's authority is derived from the power inherent in its words and teachings.

3. Biblical authority transcends _____.

4. Biblical authority is _____.

Conclusion

Let's sum up our answers to the question, Why read the Bible? First, the Bible is God's book. Since God went to miraculous lengths to give His word to us, it is clear that He intends it to be understood. Second, the Bible is a revealing book. Its purpose is to reveal our need and Christ as our answer. We study it to experience God.

Third, the Bible is an inspired book. God gave us His very words. We can trust them and should approach them with reverence and humility. Fourth, the Bible is an authoritative book. God still uses it across time and culture to bring us to a lifetransforming encounter with Himself.

Erasmus, the sixteenth-century Christian scholar, once wrote of the Bible: "These sacred Words give you the very image of Christ speaking, healing, dying, rising again and make Him so present, that were He before your eyes you would not more truly see Him."[15]

When you study this book, look for Christ in its pages, trust its truths with reverence, and obey its teachings. As you do, you will indeed meet Jesus in the Word of God. And meeting your Savior personally is the most important experience in all of life. Herein lies the purpose of the Bible, and its eternal importance.

ANSWERS

CHECK YOURSELF 1

1. "book"   2. "set apart"   3. "writings"   4. F   5. F

CHECK YOURSELF 2

1. T   2. a. in Christ; b. in the Bible; c. in our witness   3. F   4. C
5. B

CHECK YOURSELF 3

1. c, f, b, d, e, a   2. T   3. F

CHECK YOURSELF 4

1. obey   2. F   3. time   4. life-transforming

2

HOW WAS THE
BIBLE CREATED?

The Making of God's Word

The question came from nowhere. I was leading a youth Bible study one Wednesday night when a high school freshman asked me, "How do you know the Bible came from God?" The look in his eyes showed how serious he was. His father was a Sunday School teacher and leader in our church, but that wasn't good enough.

He wanted to know for himself. He explained his question: "Did the Bible just drop out of heaven? How do you know that someone didn't sit down a hundred years ago and write the whole thing? Where did it come from?"

That's a good question. A few days later at work, a friend and I got into a discussion about my faith and he asked, "Why do you trust the Bible? After all those centuries of copying, surely you don't think you have what was first written. How can you trust it today?" Another good question.

Maybe you've asked questions like these yourself, or you've tried to answer them for someone else. The fact is, not many Christians know where the Bible came from. The making of God's word is a neglected subject for some, and a real problem for others. So it's important that we discuss how God's word came to us.

Writing in Ancient Times

The first step to making the Bible seems obvious: God's word was preserved in writing. However, there's much more to this step than you might think. In the ancient world writing was an expensive, laborious process. Books had to be written and copied by hand (the first printed book wasn't completed until around A.D. 1455). The postal systems of the Roman Empire generally were restricted to government use, so the biblical authors had to find special travelers or messengers to carry their writings.

Everything about ancient books was different from today, from their languages to the ways they were produced.

The "Paper" of the Bible

The "paper" of biblical times was the papyrus reed, a thin plant which grew along the Nile River in Egypt ("paper" comes from "papyrus"). This reed was cut, unrolled, and left to dry in the sun. "Pens" were brushes made of reeds; "ink" was usually a kind of carbon-liquid glue. Papyrus was common and inexpensive, and so it was used widely in the ancient world. However, it was also brittle and decayed quickly.

Those who couldn't afford papyrus sometimes wrote on clay tablets. They also used baked pieces of pottery called "ostraicon," as well as rocks, wood, or metal. Nearly anything with a flat surface could be used. A sharp object served as a stylus or "pen"; the clay usually was inscribed, then baked to preserve the writing.

A more expensive and durable writing material was parchment. This was made from animal skins, usually sheep or goats. Parchment was perfected around 200 B.C., and was used by the wealthy. Again, reed "pens" were used.

Both papyrus and parchment were rolled onto wooden rods and made into scrolls. Around A.D. 100 people began cutting scrolls into sheets and stitching them together. This is called the "codex," the ancestor of our book.

The original books of the Bible were apparently all written on papyrus. Since papyrus decayed quickly, none of these original writings exist today. Only later, as the church grew more prosperous, could it afford parchments on which to copy the biblical books. These parchments, in codex form, are the earliest copies of the complete New Testament which we have today.

The Languages of the Bible

Three languages were used in writing the Bible. Hebrew is the oldest of the three, and the language of most of the Old Testament. It is written from right to left, with no upper or lower cases. Biblical Hebrew consisted entirely of consonants; the vowels were added centuries later.

The second language of the Bible is Aramaic, a descendant of Hebrew. It was the common language of the Jews in the latter years of the Old Testament era and was used throughout the New Testament period as well. It is found in the Old Testament in three passages: Ezra 4:8–6:18; 7:12–26; and Daniel 2:4–7:28. Although they knew and used Hebrew, Aramaic was the language which Jesus and his disciples commonly spoke. Assorted Aramaic words are found scattered throughout the New Testament (for example, "Abba" for Father in Mark 14:36).

The third biblical language is Greek. By Jesus' day Greek was the universal written language of the Roman Empire, so it was the language in which the New Testament was written. However, the Greek of the New Testament is "koine" (meaning "common") Greek, not the classical Greek of the cultured. This shows that the Bible was meant for everyone, not just the learned. William Barclay points this out:

> It is worthwhile remembering that the New Testament is written in colloquial Greek; it is written in the kind of Greek the man in the

street wrote and spoke in the first century. . . . Anything that makes the New Testament sound other than contemporary mistranslates i.[1]

Don't be concerned—you don't have to know Hebrew, Aramaic and Greek to understand God's word. Bible translators and scholars can help you here. God calls these scholars and uses their translations and commentaries because He wants you to understand His word today .

Check Yourself 1

1. Match the term on the left with the correct definition on the right.

_____ Papyrus   a. A roll made of written materials, kept on a wooden rod

_____ Parchment   b. A thin reed growing along the Nile river, unrolled and used as ancient "paper"

_____ Scroll   c. Sheets of writing materials, cut and stitched together; the ancestor to our book

_____ Codex   d. Animal skin used as writing material; more expensive

2. _____ was the written language of most of the Old Testament.

3. _____ was written in portions of the Old Testament and spoken by Jesus and His contemporaries.

4. _____ was the written language of the New Testament.

Preserving What Was Written

Once God's word was written, it had to be preserved. The originals, called the "original autographs" by scholars, were written on papyrus, which decayed easily. Therefore, they had to be copied accurately.

Fortunately, we have excellent copies of the originals. We possess copies of entire books of the Bible, as well as parts of different passages. These copies, called "manuscripts," are quite numerous, and some are nearly as old as the originals.

However, there is no unanimous agreement that any one manuscript is exactly like the original. Scholars must study these different versions, seeking the one which comes closest to what the writer actually wrote. These scholars are called "textual critics" in the positive sense of "critic": one who forms judgments according to evidence and expertise. Their study is called "textual criticism."

We possess more than five thousand various Greek manuscripts, and more than ten thousand ancient copies in other languages. It is a painstaking and crucial task to choose between them in seeking the copies most like the original writings. To organize the work, scholars classify these manuscripts by age and writing materials, whether they used upper or lower case letters, and the geographic centers where they were produced. Then they look for those manuscripts which seem to be the earliest copies and thus the basis for later copies.

The oldest portion of the Greek New Testament we possess today is known as the Chester Beatty papyrus. This is a fragment from John 18:31–33,37–38, and dates from A.D. 130.

The oldest complete New Testament manuscripts we possess today are from the fourth century. They are in very good condition and appear to be excellent copies of the originals.

As a result, we have a copy of part of the New Testament which is only forty years older than the original, and copies of the complete book which are only three hundred years older. This time "gap" between the original writings and our oldest copies, while amazingly brief by comparison to other ancient writings, nonetheless causes some people to question the reliability of our Bible today. The truth is, the amount of time between the originals and their earliest copies is not a problem but a plus for the trustworthiness of the New Testament text.

The New Testament possesses the best, most reliable manuscripts of any ancient book. A comparison of these manuscripts with those of other accepted ancient works is enlightening. Caesar's *Gallic Wars* was composed between 58 and 50 B.C.; however, our oldest manuscripts of it are nine hundred years later, and only nine or ten good copies exist. Tacitus was the most famous historian of ancient Rome.

However, of the fourteen books of his *Histories*, only four and one-half survive today; of his *Annals*, our earliest manuscripts are nine hundred years later.

The *History of Thucydides* was written around 400 B.C.; however, our earliest complete manuscript of it dates to thirteen hundred years later. And yet no historian today would suggest that we cannot trust these copies. By comparison, the earliest Greek New Testament was copied just three hundred years after it was written, with five thousand copies available from across the centuries.[2] Our New Testament can be trusted as reliable.

It is true that in our Greek New Testament there are passages for which scholars have not yet settled unanimously on the correct reading. But according to F. F. Bruce, a leading authority, "The various readings about which any doubt remains among textual critics of the New Testament affect no material question of historic fact or of Christian faith and practice."[3]

Bruce quotes Sir Frederic Kenyon to prove his point:

> The interval then between the dates of original composition and the earliest extant evidence becomes so small as to be in fact negligible, and the last foundation for any doubt that the Scriptures have come down to us substantially as they were written has now been removed. Both the authenticity and the general integrity of the books of the New Testament may be regarded as finally established.[4]

God has revealed Himself in His word, and He made certain that each generation would have that revelation to read. Because His word was copied accurately, we can trust the Bible we possess to be His word for us today.

Check Yourself 2

1. Match the term on the left with the correct definition on the right:

_____ Original autographs	a.	Copies of books of the Bible
_____ Textual critics	b.	The first writings of the Bible
_____ Manuscripts	c.	Those who study ancient copies of the Bible

2. T/F: The New Testament we have today is no more reliable than any other ancient book.

3. T/F: The questions which remain regarding the New Testament text affect no significant question of fact or faith.

THE CANON

The word "canon" comes from a Hebrew word which means "reed" or "measuring rod." Eventually the word stood for a catalog or list of books. The process by which the biblical books were chosen is called "canonization." Here's how it all happened.[5]

MAKING THE OLD TESTAMENT

From ancient times, the Jews believed that God revealed Himself in writing. The Ten Commandments are an example of this. Written revelation was given by God and collected by the Jews in three stages.

First, there was the *Law*, the religious regulations of the Jewish community. Soon the stories of early Hebrew history were included as well. The whole section was called the "Torah," meaning "instruction." It was later divided into five parts, called the "Pentateuch" for "five books," and became the first five books of our Bible. This was the first part of the Bible to be compiled by the Jews.

Law	Genesis
	Exodus
	Leviticus
	Numbers
	Deuteronomy

Next came the *Prophets*, called the "Nebiim" by the Jews. This section of the Bible included the writings of the prophets and also the history of their times.

In the Jewish arrangement of the Old Testament there are eight books in this section. The first four are called the "Former Prophets"—Joshua, Judges, 1–2 Samuel, 1–2 Kings. Notice that Samuel and Kings are combined into one book each. The last four are called the "Latter Prophets"—Isaiah, Jeremiah, Ezekiel, and the Twelve. The "Twelve" is one book composed of our twelve so-called "minor prophets." These books are called "minor" only because they are shorter. The eight books of the Jewish arrangement correspond to twenty-one in our format today.

Former	Joshua	
Prophets	Judges	
	1–2 Samuel	
	1–2 Kings	
	Isaiah	
Latter	Jeremiah	
Prophets	Ezekiel	
	The "Twelve"	Hosea
		Joel
		Amos
		Obadiah
		Jonah
		Micah
		Nahum
		Habakkuk
		Zephaniah
		Haggai
		Zechariah
		Malachi

Last came the *Writings*. These books are called the "Ketubim" by the Jews. They may have grown from smaller, earlier writings. For instance, the individual Psalms were probably used first by the Jews in worship, then later compiled into the Book of Psalms. The Jews list eleven books in this section.

Writings	Psalms
	Proverbs
	Job
	Song of Solomon
	Ruth
	Lamentations
	Ecclesiastes
	Esther
	Daniel
	Ezra-Nehemiah
	1–2 Chronicles

Notice that Ezra and Nehemiah are combined, as are 1 and 2 Chronicles. Also note that the Jewish Bible ends not with Malachi but with 2 Chronicles.

And so we have the earliest division of the Hebrew Bible: the Law, the Prophets, and the Writings. This arrangement was current in Jesus' day (see Luke 24:44). Josephus, the first-century Jewish historian, gives it as the Hebrew Bible of his day.

These books, twenty-four in the Jewish arrangement and thirty-nine in ours, were compiled over centuries of use. However, they were not formally listed and arranged until around A.D. 90. There were two reasons why this final list was created. First, the city of Jerusalem had been destroyed by the Romans in A.D. 70, and the Jews realized that they needed to preserve their Scriptures from further catastrophe. Second, the Christian writings which make up our New Testament were becoming popular. The Jews wanted to finalize their Scriptures to prevent Christian influence.

According to Jewish tradition, two councils of Jewish rabbis and scholars were held to accomplish this task. They met in A.D. 90 and 118, both at Jamnia (sometimes called Jabne) on the Mediterranean coast. Here the books of the Hebrew Bible were discussed and a proper list was created. These books are our Old Testament today.

Josephus records for us the Jews' belief concerning their Scriptures:

> We have not an unnumerable multitude of books among us, disagreeing and contradicting one another, but only twenty-two books [his arrangement is different from the more common twenty-four], which contain the records of all the past times; which are justly believed to be divine.[6]

The Jewish belief in a divine Being had led them to believe in the authority of His Book as well. We share that belief today.

CHECK YOURSELF 3

1. Match the term on the left with the correct definition on the right.

_____ Canon   a. Means "five books"

____ Torah   b. A catalog or list of books

____ Pentateuch   c. The city where councils were held which
                          created the list of Old Testament books

____ The "Twelve"   d. The so-called "minor" prophets

____ Jamnia   e. Means "instruction"

2. The Jewish arrangement of the Old Testament, current in Jesus' day, ends with the books _____.

3. The three "stages" of the Old Testament were _____, _____, and _____.

BETWEEN THE OLD AND NEW TESTAMENTS

Malachi, the last Old Testament book, was written around 400 B.C., and the first Gospels were composed around A.D. 45–50. What happened in the meanwhile?

This question raises one of the most interesting issues in the story of the biblical canon. This is the subject of the "Apocrypha," a story unfamiliar to most Protestants. The word "apocrypha" means "hidden" or "obscure." With regard to the canon, it refers to fifteen books which some accept as scriptural and others reject. Here's a brief account of these fascinating and controversial books.

The apocryphal books were probably written at the end of the Old Testament era. All are in Greek, although one—Sirach—seems to have had a Hebrew original. The Jews in Alexandria, Egypt, accepted these books as part of divine revelation. The Jews in Palestine never accepted them as Scripture, however, and they are all rejected in Judaism today.

Apocrypha	First Esdras
(in order)	First Maccabees
	Second Maccabees
	Tobit
	Judith
	Additions to the book of Esther
	The Song of the Three Young Men

> Susanna
> Bel and the Dragon
> The Wisdom of Solomon
> Wisdom of Jesus the Son of
> 　Sirach (also known as
> 　Ecclesiasticus)
> Baruch
> The Letter of Jeremiah
> The Prayer of Manasseh
> Second Esdras

Now the story shifts to a group of Jewish scholars meeting in the first century A.D. to translate the Hebrew Bible into the more-popular Greek language. This translation is known as the "Septuagint," in reference to the "seventy" translators (we'll study it in more detail in the chapter five, when we look at Bible translations). It so happens that these Jewish scholars included the apocryphal books in their translation of the Hebrew Bible, giving these books credibility and authority. Later, the Roman Catholic Church came to accept the fifteen books as part of their Bible.

Why are these books not accepted by all Christians? When the Protestant Reformation began some four hundred years ago, the reformers were convinced that the apocryphal books should be excluded. They noted that none of the books are specifically quoted anywhere in the New Testament. They also cited the more scholarly early church fathers who maintained a sharp distinction between the Hebrew Old Testament and these Greek additions.

They concluded that these books, while interesting and informative, should not be considered divine revelation. Today, Protestant Bibles exclude these books. In one sense, then, the question of the canon is not settled even today. So long as Catholics and Protestants disagree about the books of the Apocrypha, the debate over the canon of the Bible will continue.

CHECK YOURSELF 4

1.　"Apocryphal" means _____.

2. The Septuagint was a translation of the Old Testament from
   _____ into _____.

3. Who accepted the Apocrypha as Scripture? (Check all that
   apply):

   ☐ Jews in Alexandria, Egypt

   ☐ Jews in Palestine

   ☐ The Roman Catholic Church

   ☐ The Reformers

4. T/F: The Apocrypha is not accepted by Jews today.

5. T/F: The apocryphal books are quoted directly in the New
   Testament.

MAKING THE NEW TESTAMENT

Justin Martyr was one of the church's first heroes. The Romans
killed him around A.D. 165 to silence his powerful Christian witness.
His writings in defense of Christianity are some of the earliest
statements of our faith. In one of them, he gives the oldest description
of Christian worship we have today:

> On the day called Sunday, all who live in cities or in the country gather
> together to one place, and the memoirs of the apostles or the writings
> of the prophets are read, as long as time permits; then, when the reader
> has ceased, the president verbally instructs, and exhorts to the imita-
> tion of these good things.[7]

"Memoirs of the apostles" refers to our New Testament, and
"writings of the prophets" refers to our Old Testament. This means
that by the mid-second century the church had a set of writings of
the apostles of Christ in addition to the Hebrew Bible. How did this
new set of books come to exist?

In brief, this was the process:

1. The books of what we call the New Testament were written;

2. They were widely read;

3. They were accepted by the churches as useful for life and doctrine;

4. They made their way into the public worship of the church;

5. They won acceptance throughout the whole church, not just among local congregations; and

6. They were officially approved by the formal decision of the church.

Now, let's look more closely at the process by which God gave us the rest of His word by answering four important questions about the creation of the New Testament.

Why was the New Testament needed?[8] Why did Christians begin to write books at all? Jesus never wrote a book, nor did He command His followers to do so. So, why did the church need the New Testament? It's interesting to note that each reason why the first Christians needed the New Testament also shows our need for it today.

1. The church needed eyewitness accounts of Christ. The apostles and eyewitnesses to Jesus' life were beginning to pass from the scene, and the churches needed written records of their experiences and faith. All of the apostles but John died before A.D. 70. For this reason, almost immediately there was a need to preserve their witness. To meet this need, Mark recorded the preaching material which he had heard Peter use, and Luke compiled Paul's life and preaching material.[9] Matthew wrote his own gospel. According to Jerome (who died in the year 420), John did the same when he realized his own death was imminent. Other apostles also wrote letters and books. In this way, the eyewitness records about Jesus could be kept for ages to come.

This first-person authority makes the New Testament indispensable and powerful today. Here we can meet Jesus through those who knew Him personally. The eyewitnesses to the life of Christ wrote for His church, then and now.

2. The world needed the story of Jesus. The first Christians knew that the world was their mission field. They needed a written word about

Christ in order to reach it. As the gospel message was carried across the Roman Empire, it encountered a literary culture in which books were widely read. To minister in this culture, books about Christ were written. In the same way, a written account of the gospel is critical to the modern mission task. One of the first jobs of the missionary is to give the people the story of Jesus in a language they can read for themselves. Throughout Christian history, the New Testament has remained the one indispensable missionary tool.

3. *Disciples needed training.* A written word was essential to discipleship and the multiplying of believers in the first century. Wherever the gospel was planted, converts had to be trained to win their cities. Books were needed for this ongoing task as the missionaries moved on to other fields.

The most basic tool of discipleship today remains the New Testament. Only when we train our people to win and disciple others can missions by multiplication occur—and this is the only method which will reach our world for Christ. Because disciples need training, we need the New Testament today.

4. *The faith must be handed down.* Many of the first Christians believed that Jesus would return in their lifetime. As the years went by, however, they began to see that their work was for the long term, and that they needed to hand down their faith to the generations following. Eyewitnesses and those who knew their stories were passing from the scene. Written records were critical to continuing the faith.

Today the New Testament remains our written lifeline to Jesus. As each generation passes away, it can hand on its faith through God's word. The New Testament is our most important means of continuing our faith.

5. *The church needed doctrinal standards.* As the church aged and expanded, it began to meet with different ways of thinking and believing. How were Christians to know right belief from wrong? Doctrinal standards were needed, and this prompted much of the writing of the New Testament. For instance, Jerome says that Luke wrote his Gospel to correct those who had written in error about the life of Christ. And Luke seems to imply the same. As the prologue to his Gospel says, "Many have undertaken to draw up an account of the things that have been fulfilled among us," but "since I myself have carefully investigated everything from the beginning, it seemed good

also for me to write an orderly account" (Luke 1:1,3). The church needed written doctrinal standards. The New Testament was God's answer to this need.

We need these standards today, more than ever. Advances in communication technology have shrunk our world. Non-Christian religions and ideas are having a great impact on us today. The best, most objective test Christians have for separating truth from heresy is God's written word.

6. The church needed practical guidelines. In addition, early Christians needed practical help for their churches and lives. How was the church to be governed? How should they worship? By what standards should they live? These practical questions were important. The books of the New Testament, especially the letters, were written to address these pressing issues.

The New Testament remains our guideline for Christian practice today. Here we find God's will for our worship, ministry, and daily lives.

7. The church needed to explain and defend the gospel. Matthew wrote his Gospel because his people, the Jews, needed to know that Jesus was their Messiah and the fulfillment of prophecy. Mark wrote to the Romans to show them that Jesus was the Son of God. Luke wrote his Gospel to show the Gentiles that they were included in God's universal plan and love. John wrote to show the Greeks the internal logic and wisdom of the gospel. In explaining and defending the gospel, the church developed the New Testament as its written tool for ministry.

Christianity still must be explained and defended. The more we accomplish our missionary purpose, the more misunderstanding and opposition we will see. Always the primary tool for explaining and defending the faith is the word of God.

8. Jesus' words needed to be preserved. Jesus' followers had a supreme reverence for His words and teachings, and wanted none of them to be lost. As the eyewitnesses passed from the scene, preserving Jesus' words became a growing concern. As a result the Gospels and letters of our New Testament were written to record and pass on the words of our Lord. We owe the same reverence to the words of our Savior. The only authoritative place we can go to find them is the New Testament. This fact alone makes God's word of supreme value today.

9. The New Covenant required the New Testament. A "covenant" is a contract or legal arrangement. The old "covenant" was God's contract with humankind based on animal sacrifice. This sacrificial system was fulfilled in Jesus' death and resurrection. We are now under the new "covenant" with God, a contract based on grace through faith. The word "testament" is another term for "covenant" or "will." The New Testament is therefore literally our "New Covenant" with God. God gave us this book to explain our new relationship with Him through Christ.

The Christian faith is still based on God's grace, received through faith (Eph. 2:8–9). But we must know about this grace before we can receive it. God's grace "covenant" is made known to us today through the new covenant, the New Testament.

The New Testament was needed in the first century and is still indispensable today. The reasons God gave us His word two thousand years ago are the same reasons He preserved it for us today.

Check Yourself 5

The New Testament was needed because:

1. The church needed _____ accounts of the life and teachings of Jesus.

2. The world needed the _____ of Jesus.

3. Disciples needed _____.

4. The faith must be _____ to the generations to come.

5. The church needed _____ standards.

6. The church needed practical _____.

7. The church needed to _____ and _____ the gospel.

8. Jesus' words must be _____.

9. The New _____ required the New Testament.

Why was the process so long? The need for the New Testament raises a second question: If these books were so vital, why did it take so long for them to be written and compiled? The first time we find a list of New Testament books like ours today is A.D. 367. It took more than three hundred years for the New Testament to reach this final form.

Why this delay in completing and compiling the New Testament?

There were five reasons:

1. The first Christians used the Old Testament for their new faith and saw no immediate need for additional writings. They knew that the Old Testament was fulfilled in Christ. And they had ways of interpreting it which helped them to find Jesus on every page.

For example, you may remember Rahab's scarlet rope which she hung from the window of her home in Jericho before the fall of that city (see Josh. 2:1–21). Here's how this passage was interpreted by Clement, pastor of the church in Rome, companion of Paul and contemporary with John:

> Moreover, they gave her a sign to this effect, that she should hang forth from her house a scarlet thread. And thus they made it manifest that redemption should flow through the blood of the Lord to all them that believe and hope in God. You see, beloved, that there was not only faith, but prophecy, in this woman.[10]

The first believers made the Old Testament their book about Christ. But as they began to reach those unfamiliar with the Old Testament, and as they began to need a more direct word for their churches, these early Christians began to write and compile the New Testament.

2. The first church developed in a non-literary situation. In Palestine the Jews transmitted their faith orally rather than in written form. Copying books was extremely expensive, out of the reach of most Christians. In addition, while some of the first believers were highly educated (Paul and Luke, for example), many were not. As Paul says, "Brothers, think of what you were when you were called. Not many of you were wise by human standards; not many were influential; not many were of noble birth" (1 Cor. 1:26). But as the church expanded into the larger literary world, Christians then produced writings about their faith.

3. The original apostles were eyewitnesses to Christ and thus the "living books" of the church. Only when they began to pass from the scene did they and their followers record their experiences and faith.

4. The first Christians believed that Jesus would return immediately. Why record the faith for posterity when there would be no one to read these records? As Jesus' coming was delayed, they began to turn to the task of handing their faith on to coming generations.

5. The New Testament was in fact written and compiled by the people long before the completed canon was officially recognized. The final list of New Testament books which was recognized in A.D. 367 only formalized what the church had been practicing for generations. The New Testament was complete in faith and practice long before the canon was officially closed. The Lord gave His word as His people needed it. There were no unnecessary or harmful delays in this process. The Lord's timing, like His word, is trustworthy.

Check Yourself 6

The process of writing the New Testament was delayed because:

1. The first Christians used the _____ _____ for their faith.

2. The first church lived in a _____ situation.

3. The original apostles were eyewitnesses to Christ and thus the "_____ _____" of the church.

4. The first Christians believed that Jesus would return _____.

5. The New Testament was written and compiled long before the completed _____ was officially recognized.

How were the proper books chosen? Books indeed came to be written about Christ and His church.

But which of these were inspired by the Lord and which were merely about Him? Many "life of Christ" volumes were circulating, as were many letters. Which of these should be accepted by the church as God's direct revelation? Which books should be read in church services? Which books could and could not be handed over to persecuting Roman authorities without sin? These were intensely practical questions in the first centuries of Christianity.

Eventually, four standards of acceptance grew up:

1. A book must have been written by an apostle or based on his eyewitness testimony. The apostles were both personal eyewitnesses of Christ's ministry and the first leaders in His church. Their witness became the first authority in this new community of faith.[11] Thus *Matthew* and *John* came to be accepted because they were written by apostles. *Mark* was influenced by Peter, and *Luke* and *Acts* were associated with the life and work of Paul. Paul's letters bore his apostolic authority, as did those of James, Peter, and John. Jude was accepted as coming from Jesus' half-brother. *Revelation* was associated with the apostle John as well. When *Hebrews* came to be linked to Paul (probably erroneously), then it was accepted into the canon.

2. A book must possess merit and authority in its use. Certain books simply proved more helpful than others for church reading, worship, and Christian living. To read the books which eventually came to be included in the New Testament, and then to read the books and letters which were left out, is to see the difference. An ancient book titled *The First Gospel of the Infancy of Jesus Christ* tells of a man changed into a mule by a bewitching spell but converted back to manhood when the infant Christ is put on his back for a ride (7:5–27). In the same book the boy Jesus causes clay birds and animals to come to life (ch. 15), stretches a throne his father had made too small (ch. 16), and takes the lives of boys who oppose him (19:19–24). These kinds of mythical stories are common in those books and letters the church wisely excluded from Scripture.

3. A book must be accepted by the entire church. Authors usually had a following in their own church and community, but only those books used by the entire church came to be included in the canon. As pastors and members of the various congregations communicated with each other, the books being used most widely became obvious.

4. The book must be approved by the decision of the church. This was done by the official church councils, as we will soon see.

Here's how the process worked. The first books of the New Testament to be collected and used widely were the letters of Paul. Peter makes a fascinating reference to them:

[Paul] writes the same way in all his letters, speaking in them of these matters. His letters contain some things that are hard to understand, which ignorant and unstable people distort, as they do the other Scriptures, to their own destruction. (2 Pet. 3:16)

By this time, Paul's writings were obviously considered "Scripture." The oldest non-biblical letters also make repeated references to Paul's letters. By at least A.D. 100, Paul's works were collected together and used widely.

Next came the Gospels. Soon after the death and resurrection of Jesus, many "life of Christ" writings began to appear. Among them was the *Protevangelion*, purporting to supply details of the birth of Christ; two books on the infancy of Christ, one claiming to be written by the apostle Thomas; and the *Gospel of Nicodemus*, sometimes referred to as the *Acts of Pontius Pilate*. However, by the mid-second century only Matthew, Mark, Luke and John were accepted universally by the church. The other "gospels" simply did not meet the four criteria for acceptance set out above.

At a very early date, all four of these canonical Gospels were united into one collection and called "The Gospel." As early as A.D. 115 Ignatius, bishop of Antioch, refers to them in this combined way. Around 170 an Assyrian Christian named Tatian composed one continuous narrative or "harmony" of the Gospels, using only these four. And Irenaeus, bishop of Lyons in Gaul around 180, refers to the four Gospels as firmly established in the church.

Acts was always recognized as the sequel to Luke. When the four Gospels were put together as a unit, Acts was placed after them in order, but it was always accepted by the church as part of the canon.

The rest of the New Testament was chosen through different processes. 1 Peter and 1 John were seldom questioned. Hebrews was accepted after it was connected with Paul. When the authorship of 2 Peter, 2 and 3 John, James, Jude and Revelation was settled, these books were placed on the list as well.

And so the books of the New Testament were chosen by the church on the basis of their authors' authority and their practical benefits. Because they still possess this authority and benefit, we need no others today.

Who finalized the canon? The first attempt to choose the New Testament books was made by Marcion of Sinope, a heretic who was expelled from the church at Rome in A.D. 144 because of his views on Jews and the Bible. Marcion hated the Jews; thus he rejected the Old Testament as the product of an inferior God. In its place he sought to establish an exclusively "Christian" canon. At the same time, he nearly worshiped Paul because of the apostle's insistence upon grace over law. In fact, his love for Paul's work actually caused some to question Paul's letters, since they were used by this heretic. Marcion accepted Luke's gospel since it was the only one not written by a Jew, although he purged many parts from it. His work resulted in this partial New Testament canon: Luke (in edited form) and ten letters of Paul (First and Second Timothy and Titus were left out).

Of course the church never accepted Marcion's canon as legitimate. This false canon did, however, raise two issues. First, which books were legitimately God's word? And second, how could the church protect Paul's letters from misuse like Marcion's in the future? To address the first issue, church leaders began to study the question of the canon. To deal with the second issue, churches began to place *Acts* before Paul's letters. In this way they gave authenticity to Paul's writings by describing first his apostolic ministry.

Soon other, more widely-accepted lists of New Testament books began to appear. One of the earliest is called the "Muratorian Fragment," since it was first published in Italy in 1740 by Cardinal L. A. Muratori. It probably represents the usage of the church at Rome around A.D. 200. This list omits James, 1 and 2 Peter, 3 John, and Hebrews, although these were soon included in later canons.[12] Another list was made by Cyril of Jerusalem (died 386), containing all of the current New Testament but Revelation. The New Testament canon which finally won approval throughout the church was set forth by Athanasius, bishop of Alexandria, in A.D. 367. In his Easter letter of that year, the bishop endeavored to "set before you the books included in the Canon, and handed down, and accredited as Divine." His statement is of such importance to the history of the New Testament that we should read it in full:

Again it is not tedious to speak of the [books] of the New Testament. These are, the four Gospels, according to Matthew, Mark, Luke, and John. Afterwards, the Acts of the Apostles and Epistles (called Catholic), seven, viz. of James, one; of Peter, two; of John, three; after these, one of Jude. In addition, there are fourteen Epistles of Paul, written in this order. The first, to the Romans; then two to the Corinthians;

after these, to the Galatians; next, to the Ephesians; then to the Philippians; next to the Colossians; after these, two to the Thessalonians, and that to the Hebrews; and again, two to Timothy; one to Titus; and lastly, that to Philemon. And besides, the Revelation of John.

These are fountains of salvation, that they who thirst may be satisfied with the living words they contain. In these alone is proclaimed the doctrine of godliness. Let no man add to these, neither let him take ought from these.[13]

This list was later approved by church councils meeting at Hippo Regius in 393 and Carthage in 397, and it remains our New Testament canon today.

Still one might ask, Did church leaders choose the books of the Bible or did God? The books of our New Testament did not become authoritative for God's people because they came to be included on a list. They were included on that list because God's people saw that they were inspired by the Lord. No one created the books or list of the Bible. God gave both, and His people simply recognized this fact.

F. F. Bruce makes this point well: "What [the church] councils did was not to impose something new upon the Christian communities but to codify what was already the general practice of those communities."[14] And Barclay agrees: "The Bible and the books of the Bible came to be regarded as the inspired word of God, not because of any decision of any Synod or Council or Committee or Church, but because in them mankind found God."[15]

CHECK YOURSELF 7

1. Match the term on the left with the correct definition on the right.

_____ Ignatius

a. New Testament canon, representing usuage at Rome around A.D. 200

_____ Marcion of Sinope

b. Bishop who sent out the canon still accepted today

____ Muratorian Fragment   c. Referred to the four Gospels as the "Gospel" in A.D. 115

____ Athanasius   d. Heretic; created the first canon

2. A book must have been written by or based on an _____.

3. A book must possess merit and _____ in its use.

4. A book must be accepted by the _____ church.

5. Which is more correct? (circle your answer)

    a. The books of the New Testament became authoritative for God's people since they were included on the official canon list.

    b. They were included on the canon list because the people already saw that they were inspired of God.

From ancient languages and manuscripts, to thousands of copies, to compiling and recognizing the sixty-six books which are God's word—the entire process was blessed by God. The One who inspired the Bible also preserved it for us. Barclay was right: the more you know about the Bible, the greater the Bible becomes.

Answers

Check Yourself 1

1. b, d, a, c   2. Hebrew   3. Aramaic   4. Greek

Check Yourself 2

1. b, c, a   2. F   3. T

Check Yourself 3

1. b, e, a, d, c   2. 1–2 Chronicles   3. Law, Prophets, and Writings

CHECK YOURSELF 4

1. "Hidden" or "obscure"   2. Hebrew into Greek   3. Jews in Alexandria; the Roman Catholic Church   4. T   5. F

CHECK YOURSELF 5

1. eyewitness   2. story   3. training   4. handed down   5. doctrinal   6. guidelines   7. explain and defend   8. preserved   9. Covenant

CHECK YOURSELF 6

1. Old Testament   2. non-literary   3. "living books"   4. immediately   5. canon

CHECK YOURSELF 7

1. c, d, a, b   2. apostle   3. authority   7. entire   8. B

3

WHY DO WE NEED
TO INTERPRET
THE BIBLE?

The Challenge of God's Word

G od said it, I believe it, and that settles it." "I may not
understand the Bible, but I believe it." "You don't have to
interpret the Bible. Just read it and do what it says." Seminary students made these kinds of statements each semester I taught
a course on biblical interpretation, and I've heard them from members of my church as well.

They all come down to one common, practical question: Why
can't we simply read the Bible and understand it the way it is? Why
do we need to interpret the Bible? "God said it, I believe it, that settles
it." Great! But what does a parent do when the Bible says, "Anyone
who curses his father or mother must be put to death" (Ex. 21:17)?
What about dietary laws such as Lev. 11:7–8: "The pig . . . is unclean

for you. You must not eat their meat or touch their carcasses; they are unclean for you"?

In the Bible King Saul visits a medium (1 Sam. 28); should we today? The Bible lists six wives of King David (2 Sam. 3:2–5); is this "biblical" now? Or do these passages need more study? One of Job's friends offered this explanation for Job's suffering: "Who, being innocent, has ever perished? Where were the upright ever destroyed?" As I have observed, those who plan evil and those who sow trouble reap it." (Job 4:7–8). Does this passage teach that suffering is always our fault? In other words, if we would just repent and believe, would we always be well and wealthy? Or, do we need to study further?

And just because an interpretation is popular, that doesn't make it right. Consider these examples.[1] After chloroform was developed in England, doctors wanted to use it to help women with childbirth. However, women refused because of Gen. 3:16—"with pain you will give birth to children." Only when it was shown from Gen. 2:21 that God "caused the man to fall into a deep sleep" to create woman would women accept chloroform.

When the first oil wells were dug in Pennsylvania, many ministers opposed this project. They argued from 2 Pet. 3:10,12 that this would deplete the oil stored in the earth for the final burning of the world. Winnowing fans were rejected for years on the basis of John 3:8 as interfering with God: "The wind blows wherever it pleases."

And a very famous sermon was preached against the woman's hair style called the "top knot." It was entitled "Top Knot Come Down"; the text was Matt. 24:17 (KJV), "Let him which is on the housetop not come down." As you can see, it's possible to be sincere and yet sincerely wrong. Nowhere is this more true than in studying the Bible.

WHAT IS BIBLICAL INTERPRETATION?

What does it mean to "interpret" the Bible? Webster defines "interpret" as "to explain the meaning of; make understandable." Interpreting the Bible, then, is understanding and explaining what the Bible means. This was the aim of one of my seminary professors as he prayed before each class, "Lord, teach us today what Your word says, and what it means by what it says."

When you interpret the Bible, you are doing biblical "hermeneutics." "Hermeneutics" is the term scholars use for interpreting any kind of language. The word itself comes from Hermes, the Greek god who was believed to bring the words of the gods to mortals. He was for them the god of science, invention, eloquence, speech, writing, and art. From then to now "hermeneutics" has been the study of language and speech.

Biblical hermeneutics is a more specific field—the study of the meaning of the language of the Bible. Its task is to determine what a biblical statement meant to its author and his readers, and then to explain and apply this meaning for us today. Don't miss the order of priority: first what the Bible meant, then what it means. The simple fact is, *the text can never mean what it never meant.*

Remembering that one fact would prevent most of the mistakes people make in understanding the Bible today. Biblical interpretation is both a science and an art. It is a science because it is guided by principles within a system. There are guidelines which will help you to understand and apply every part of the Bible. But biblical interpretation is also an art because you must apply these principles by skill.

There are two categories of guidelines for Bible study: "general" and "special." "General" principles apply to the study of every passage in the Bible. You should always know what you can about the author of the book you're studying, his times, his readers, and his purpose. This is true of every passage in Scripture. "Special" principles apply only to certain parts of the Bible. For instance, there are guidelines for interpreting the poetry of the Psalms which you wouldn't want to use in studying the historical narrative of Acts.

To sum up: biblical interpretation is our effort to understand what the Bible meant when it was written, and then to understand and live out its meaning today. This task is done through the skillful application of principles which apply to all the Bible as well as guidelines which are intended only for certain parts of Scripture.

CHECK YOURSELF 1

1. Biblical _____ is the study of the meaning of the language of the Bible; another word for "interpretation."

2. The order of priority in Bible study: first what the Bible
    _____, then what it _____.

3. "General" principles apply to _____ the Bible.

4. "Special" principles apply to _____ the Bible.

Why Does the Bible Need Interpreting?

Communication and interpretation are important subjects in our society. The biggest problem in most troubled homes is communication—learning how to share and understand each other's needs. Likewise, lawyers interpret the law for their clients; judges interpret the law for the lawyers; and police interpret the law for our citizens. Counselors help families interpret their problems.

But when we turn to the Bible, interpretation seems less necessary. Why can't we just read it? Why must it be interpreted? There are five answers to this important question.

The Lord Calls Us to Bible Study

First, the Lord wants us to interpret His word and to do this well. Paul's command to Timothy is still God's word for us today: "Do your best to present yourself to God as one approved, a workman who does not need to be ashamed and who correctly handles the word of truth" (2 Tim. 2:15). Paul's phrase "correctly handles" refers to a stone mason who cuts stones precisely so they will fit into their places in a building. We are called to interpret correctly the "word of truth."

Biblical Characters Interpret the Bible

From the time God first began to give us His word, His people have interpreted and applied it to their lives. For instance, the Ten Commandments in Exodus 20 are followed by thirty-seven chapters which interpret and apply them (Exodus 21–30 and Leviticus). The Book of Deuteronomy is Moses' interpretation and application of God's word for the Hebrews before they entered the Promised Land.

The prophets interpreted God's Law for the people and challenged them to obey it. Ezra's ministry focused on interpretation: "They read from the Book of the Law of God, making it clear and giving the meaning so that the people could understand what was being read" (Neh. 8:8). Those in the New Testament continued this practice. As Jesus taught, He interpreted the Old Testament and applied its message to Himself. When He met with two disciples following His resurrection, here was His approach:

"Beginning with Moses and all the Prophets, he explained to them what was said in all the Scriptures concerning himself" (Luke 24:27).

The Gospels each interpret Jesus' ministry. Acts describes the work of the early church to interpret the gospel for the world. The epistles interpret this gospel for the church. Revelation interprets and applies the hope of the Christian faith for all believers. The Bible not only reveals to us God's word—many of its pages are given to interpreting and applying that word as well. Bible study is itself "biblical."

THE BIBLE IS GOD'S AUTHORITATIVE WORD

Another reason the Bible must be interpreted and understood is because of its importance in our lives. As we saw in chapter 1, the Bible is God's book. It shows us that we need Him and that He will meet us in His word. It is His authority for our lives today. Protestants from the first called the Bible the "sola fidei regula," our only rule of faith. We *must* understand and apply its message faithfully to our lives.

The Bible is God's word of authority on every spiritual topic. The way we interpret it will govern how we understand salvation, the Christian life, and every other spiritual issue. We must interpret it properly so that we can know God's word on these subjects. His authoritative word merits our best efforts to study its truths.

THE BIBLE IS AN ANCIENT BOOK

One fact about the Bible which we often overlook is that it is a very old book. Its authors finished writing during the days of the Roman Empire. Their words were being read five hundred years before the Middle Ages, fourteen hundred years before Columbus, and seventeen hundred years before the founding of America. The Bible was written for a very different society from ours.

We must understand what the Bible meant then so we can know what it means today. There are four "gaps" between biblical times and ours. For each "gap," interpretation is the bridge we need for the biblical message to cross over to us.[2]

The Time Gap. We are separated from biblical events by thousands of years. It makes sense that the more we close this gap in time, the better we can understand the Bible.

For instance, we can understand Jonah's refusal to go to Nineveh and preach against their sins when we know about these sins. The Ninevites were a warrior nation, so cruel that they often peeled the skin from those they conquered and used it as wallpaper in their homes. Understanding the times helps us identify with Jonah's struggle to be faithful. Crossing the time gap brings home the biblical message.

The Culture Gap. We also need to understand the differences between the culture of the biblical times and ours. Consider Jesus' statement, "If someone forces you to go one mile, go with him two miles" (Matt. 5:41). He was referring to the law which permitted Roman soldiers to force their subjects to carry their military pack for one mile. This was an act of slavery and terrible humiliation. Jesus calls us to respond to humiliation with willing service.

Another example is Jesus' warning, "Do not store up for yourselves treasures on earth, where moth and rust destroy, and where thieves break in and steal" (Matt. 6:19). In Jesus' day a man often buried his money beneath a wall of his house.

These walls were thin and brittle, and thieves could simply put their fist through and steal what was buried beneath. Jesus is saying that earthly possessions can be stolen, no matter where we hide them, so we should invest in heaven instead. Once we cross the culture gap, we understand the relevance and power of God's word.

The Language Gap. Differences in the meaning of words and expressions often confuse us as we study. Consider this perplexing statement by Jesus: "Anyone who says to his brother, 'Raca,' is answerable to the Sanhedrin. But anyone who says, 'You fool!' will be in danger of the fire of hell" (Matt. 5:22). "Raca" was an Aramaic term of contempt, something similar to an obscenity today.

"Fool" was even worse, however, for this word accused a person of immorality in character. What Jesus is saying is that using an obscenity is wrong and punishable, but slandering someone's character is even worse. When we cross the language gap we understand that obscenity and slander are both wrong today.

The Perspective Gap. People in biblical times had ways of understanding their world which are sometimes much different from ours. For instance, they could speak of the "four quarters of the earth" (Isa. 11:12). They thought of heaven as "up" (Job 22:12; Rev. 4:1) and hell as "down" (Prov. 15:24; see Job 11:8). Theirs was simply a pre-scientific understanding of God's creation.

Now, this does not make them any less intelligent than us. Our own understanding of the universe continues to change and contradict our earlier beliefs. Newton's "laws" have become Einstein's "theories," and we learn more every day about the wonder and complexity of God's world. Nonetheless, we must watch for places in Scripture where the author and his first readers viewed the world in ways which must be interpreted for people today. When we cross the perspective gap we can apply the message found within the biblical world-view.

The Bible does not need to be *made* relevant. Human nature does not change, so the biblical answers to our problems do not change either. But we must clear the way for the message of the Bible to be understood today. We must help people cross the "gaps" between themselves and God's word. When we build these bridges the biblical message will come across in its ever-relevant power.[3]

You Must Understand the Author's Intended Meaning

God has one primary purpose for His word: to bring us into personal relationship with Himself. This purpose must always be kept in mind as you are studying the Scriptures. Along with this general purpose, however, there is also a specific purpose for each individual passage. You must know what the author intended to say if his work is to make sense today. Here we find one of the most important principles for all Bible study: *you must know what the author meant before you can know what his words mean now.*

The Bible can never mean what it never meant. You must apply the Scriptures in keeping with their intended meaning and purpose. This raises a very difficult problem for modern readers: how can you know the author's intent? How do you decide what Matthew wanted to accomplish with his Gospel, or the reasons why Moses gave us Leviticus? There's only one answer to this problem: interpretation. Principles of Bible study can help you understand the purpose behind each part of the Bible. Then you can apply the passage in the way its author intended. This makes for life-changing study of God's word.

WHY MUST *You* INTERPRET THE BIBLE?

If we believe in the task and necessity of biblical interpretation, one more question naturally arises: why must *you* learn to do this? Isn't this what you expect your pastor to do? When you're sick you consult a doctor. When you need to travel by air you trust a pilot. Why then do you need to learn how to interpret the Bible for yourself? Can't you simply rely on your pastor and other professionals to do this for you? Gordon MacDonald, one of the most insightful pastors of our generation, says, "No!" Here's his explanation:

> [Pastors] spend too much time studying the Bible for their people. . . . Frankly, one of my greatest personal regrets in twenty-five years of preaching is that I don't feel I taught my people how to study the Bible for themselves, either as individuals or in a group. I think I've been a fairly good preacher. People took notes and were very affirming about what I preached. So I think my preaching was definitely meeting a need. But now as I look back, I feel I was studying the Bible for the people. We are moving toward a point where there are just a few strong communicators who are studying the Bible for us all. What I should have done was help them to understand how I studied it and how they could learn to study it for themselves.[4]

MacDonald is right, for three reasons.

GOD WANTS TO MEET YOU PERSONALLY IN HIS WORD

God intends the Bible to draw you into personal fellowship with Him. He cannot do this when you study His word only through the mind and personality of another person. The Bible becomes a sec-ond-hand book for you. You are drawn more to the preacher than to the person of Christ, and this is not the intention of the Scripture. Jesus cannot be experienced second-hand. Salvation is intensely personal in nature. The Holy Spirit dwells personally in your heart. Spiritual growth is a matter of personal, individual experience.

Nothing God intends the Bible to accomplish in your life can be done effectively second-hand. Now, this doesn't mean that you don't need the assistance of other Christians. Those who have devoted their lives to the study of the Bible have much help to offer you. The Christian life was always meant to be lived in community with other believers. This is true of Bible study as well. The point is, you must not depend on others. You must interpret God's word for yourself if the purpose of Bible study is to be fulfilled in your life.

You Have the Right to Study for Yourself

Each Christian is his or her own priest before God. We call this doctrine "the priesthood of the believer." This means that you need no intermediary between yourself and your Father. You can pray directly to God, confess your sins and ask His forgiveness, and live in personal fellowship with Him.

One very important result of this doctrine is that every believer has the right and responsibility to interpret the Bible personally. As you need no intermediary between you and God, so you need none between you and His word. The same Holy Spirit who brought salvation to your heart can bring the truth of Scripture to your mind. Since you are your own priest before God, you can learn His word for yourself.

You Should Not Depend on the Opinions of Others

A third, very important reason why you should learn to study the Bible for yourself is that if you don't, your ideas will be those of others. And the opinions of others are not always right. If you let others do all your Bible study for you, you will only know God as they do. Their opinions and biases, however good or bad, will become yours. It is impossible to interpret the Bible with absolute objectivity. No one can interpret the Bible apart from his or her own presuppositions. Our opinions will always affect our Bible study.

Religious heritage affects Bible study, for the doctrines of our church usually become our own. Take Jesus' word to Peter, "You are Peter, and on this rock I will build my church" (Matt. 16:18). Catholic interpreters will see in this text the establishment of the papacy; Protestants will not. Each brings his or her own religious heritage and viewpoint to the text.

Logically-oriented people tend to make the Bible very rational and systematic, drawing charts and lining up texts in logical order. Practically-oriented people often make the Bible a handbook for personal accomplishment, a book of "how to's" for marriage, family, finances, government, and so on. Those who are influenced heavily by the scientific method may have a hard time with biblical miracles. An evolutionist will obviously interpret Genesis differently from a creationist. Those who believe that "speaking in tongues" ceased with the first century will approach 1 Corinthians 12 and 14 very differently than those who affirm tongues today.

If one believes that women should not preach, this will clearly affect his or her interpretation of Acts 21:9: "[Philip] had four unmarried daughters who prophesied." At every turn, personal opinions affect Bible study. The following shows how the opinions of people can affect every part of the process of Bible study:

> ➪ The Original Biblical Writings (none in existence today)
> ➪ Copies (made, compiled, and edited by people)
> ➪ Translations (made by people)
> ➪ Commentaries (written by people)
> ➪ Sermons (given by people)
> ➪ Congregation (heard by people)

As you can see, the closer you get to the original text, the less you will inherit the presuppositions of others.

God wants to meet you personally in His word, but for this to occur you must interpret it yourself. You are your own priest before the Father, but you must interpret the Bible for yourself to exercise this privilege and responsibility. In the Bible God wants to speak directly to you, but you must interpret His word for yourself or else your beliefs will largely be those of others. You need to learn and apply principles which make the Bible God's word to *you*.

CHECK YOURSELF 2

Why the Bible requires interpretation:

1. The _____ call us to Bible study.

2. _____ _____ interpret the Bible.

3. The Bible is God's _____ word.

4. The Bible is an _____ book.

5. You must understand the author's _____ meaning.

Why you must interpret the Bible personally:

6. God wants to meet you _____ in His word.

7. You have the right to study _____.

8. You should not depend on the _____ of others.

9. Match the category on the left with its best example on the right:

   ____ Time gap   a. "If someone forces you to go one mile, go with him two."

   ____ Culture gap   b. The "four quarters of the earth"

   ____ Language gap   c. Jonah's refusal to confront the sin of the wicked Ninevites

   ____ Perspective gap   d. "Raca"

One Last Word

This book is intended to help you make the Bible God's personal word for you. One caution, however: the true Teacher of God's word is the Lord Himself. You must use the principles in this book by the guidance of the Holy Spirit. This book is only a means to an end. God wants to use these principles by His Spirit to help you meet Him in His word.

Martin Luther, the man who most inspired the Protestant Reformation of four hundred years ago, was firmly aware of his dependence on God's Spirit in knowing God's truth. I have his "Pastoral Prayer" on my office wall and read it often. Let us make his prayer ours today:

O Lord God, Thou hast made me a pastor and teacher in the church. Thou seest how unfit I am to administer rightly this great responsible office; and had I been without Thy aid and counsel I would surely have ruined it all long ago. Therefore do I invoke Thee. How gladly do I desire to yield and consecrate my heart and mouth to this ministry! I desire to teach the congregation. I, too, desire ever to learn and to keep Thy word my constant companion and to meditate thereupon earnestly. Use me as Thy instrument in Thy service. Only do not Thou forsake me, for if I am left to myself, I will certainly bring it all to destruction. Amen.

Answers

Check Yourself 1

1. hermeneutics   2. meant, means   3. all   4. parts of

Check Yourself 2

1. Lord   2. Biblical characters   3. authoritative   4. ancient
5. intended   6. personally   7. for yourself   8. opinions   9. c, a, d, b

4

WHAT IS THE BIBLE ABOUT?

The Main Ideas of God's Word

There is an old story about the Sunday morning when President Truman went to church alone. His wife was ill and couldn't go with him, so she wanted all the details about the service. The President wasn't much help. He couldn't remember the names of the hymns; he didn't recall the music the choir sang; he didn't know who had joined the church that day. Finally in exasperation his wife asked, "What did the pastor preach on?" "Sin," Truman replied. "What did he say?" "He was against it." That was enough.

To understand a sermon, you must know what it's about. In the same way, it is vital to know what a book is about—to know its message, its organization, and its purpose. When you're familiar with the author's theme and you know how the parts of the book fit together, you can read with much greater insight.

So let's ask some important questions about the Bible: Who is its central figure? What is its central theme? What are its books about? How do they relate to each other? We often overlook these questions in Bible study, to our loss. We tend to study individual parts of the Bible without relating them to the whole, thus missing their larger meaning and purpose. The answer to the vital question, "What is the Bible about?" comes in four parts.

Who Is the Central Figure of the Bible?

One of the most dramatic events in Scripture occurs late on Easter Sunday, on the road to the village Emmaus. Two of Jesus' disciples are walking the seven miles home from Jerusalem. Their hearts are broken with sorrow, their steps heavy with grief.

Jesus, the one they were certain was God's Son and Savior, is dead. Now they've heard that even His body has disappeared. All trace of Him is gone, and their world has crashed in on them in despair and defeat. Suddenly, Jesus joins them on the way.

"What are you discussing together as you walk along?" He asks. They tell Him of their grief at the death of their Lord, and their confusion about His empty tomb. And then, in one of the focal passages of the entire Bible, Jesus replies to them, "How foolish you are, and how slow of heart to believe all that the prophets have spoken! Did not the Christ have to suffer these things and then enter His glory?" And then, "beginning with Moses and all the Prophets, He explained to them what was said in all the Scriptures concerning Himself" (Luke 24:25–27).

Here Jesus unveils the central focus of the Bible: Himself. He is the fulfillment of Moses, the Prophets, and the Old Testament. He is the hero of the New Testament. The central figure of the Bible is Jesus Christ. This fact makes the Bible "Christocentric"—Christ is its center. This principle cannot be overemphasized, for it alone makes the books of the Bible into the Book. A. J. Conyers notes,

> No one before had dared to propose that Scripture had a central figure. Abraham, Moses, Samuel, David and Elijah were figures of impressive stature in the history of Israel, but none of them could be said to be the central figure. Christians, however, were impressed that all of the loose strands of prophecy, all of the straying tendencies of history, and all of the vast hopes of Israel were summed up in God's

self-disclosure in Jesus Christ. If the book of the Jews was only a collection before this time, now it became welded into a unity. The New Testament witness to the Incarnation of the Son of God made it one book.[1]

Without Christ at its center, the Bible can be a very confusing book. Written over twelve hundred years by at least forty-three authors, its basic ideas can be difficult to grasp. But when you understand that the Scriptures are focused and fulfilled in Jesus, this brings the parts of the Bible into a whole. Let's see how Christ is the central figure of God's word.

JESUS FULFILLS THE OLD TESTAMENT

We'll begin with the Old Testament. For many Christians, its purpose is confusing at best. Why do we need these ancient laws, histories, and rituals? What significance can they possibly have for us?

The answer can be stated simply. Jesus gave us both the purpose and the relevance of the Old Testament in one sentence: "Do not think that I have come to abolish the Law or the Prophets; I have not come to abolish them but to fulfill them" (Matt. 5:17). In saying this, Jesus tells us that the Old Testament is still the word of God. It is neither abolished nor irrelevant. And He also shows us that the message and meaning of the Old Testament is fulfilled in Himself. When we read these books as preparations for Christ, we find in them relevant principles for following Him today.

First, consider the Laws of the Old Testament. Here you find everything from rules about diet to ways to handle skin infections. Why this multitude of detailed laws which no one could ever keep perfectly? This question was in the heart of every Jew. Here's the answer:

> Before this faith came [in Christ], we were held prisoners by the law, locked up until faith could be revealed. So the law was put in charge to lead us to Christ that we might be justified by faith (Gal. 3:23–24).

God gave the Jews the law to show them their need for grace in Jesus. By giving them His law for perfect living, He showed them how imperfect and fallen they were. He proved that they needed to be saved from their sins. And now Christ the Savior fulfills the law.

The Old Testament sacrificial systemincludes regulations for sacrifices for every kind of sin. What possible relevance could this have for us today? The answer is that the system of animal sacrifice prepared the people to understand Jesus' sacrifice at Calvary. The concept behind blood sacrifice was: by grace God would "transfer" the sins of His people to an innocent animal, and then "punish" that animal by death. In this way God's people could be forgiven and restored to Him.

However, no animal could truly take away our sin. The animal sacrifices were but a preparation for the death of Christ, the only effective answer to the sin of mankind. And so at Calvary, "God made him who had no sin to be sin for us, so that in him we might become the righteousness of God" (2 Cor. 5:21). Jesus' death now fulfills all sacrifice for us (Heb. 10:11–14).

Third, consider the history of Israel. Why all these stories of ancient battles and conquests, kings and nations? Many relevant principles can be found in these narratives. However, God's chief reason for creating Israel was to bring through it His Son. This is the best way to understand the significance of the nation and its history.

For this reason Matthew's Gospel, written for the Jews, begins with the genealogy of Jesus to show that He is the fulfillment of the Jewish nation. Beginning with Abraham, the father of the Jews, Matthew traces his people to Jesus, their Savior and Lord. The history of Israel is "His story." Christ also fulfills the wisdom literature and the prophets.

The wisdom books (Job to the Song of Solomon) taught the Hebrews how to approach everyday living by faith and obedience. They are best interpreted through faith in Him who is "the way and the truth and the life" (John 14:6). The prophets pointed the way ultimately to Jesus, God's Son: "In the past God spoke to our forefathers through the prophets at many times and in various ways, but in these last days He has spoken to us by His Son, whom He appointed heir of all things, and through whom He made the universe" (Heb. 1:1–2).

So we can conclude that the Old Testament is best read through the lens of faith in Jesus Christ. When we approach it in this way, its principles and preparations lead us to a deepened faith and disciplined obedience. Jesus fulfills the Old Testament as the central figure of the word of God.

JESUS IS THE FOCUS OF THE NEW TESTAMENT

The earliest preaching of the Christian church built on the fact that Christ fulfilled the Old Testament as the Son of God. Consider Peter's message at Pentecost, the first sermon of the church (Acts 2:14–40). The outline of his message is simple, and it centers in Christ: (1) salvation in Jesus fulfills the promise of the Old Testament (vv. 17–21; see Joel 2:28–32);(2) Jesus is real (v. 22); (3) He died on the cross (v. 23); (4) He rose from the grave (v. 24); (5) His death and resurrection fulfill the Old Testament promise of the coming Holy One (vv. 25–32; see Ps. 16:8–11); (6) Jesus is now Lord (vv. 33–36); (7) you must receive him as your personal savior (vv. 38–40).

Paul's preaching follows the same approach. In his message to the Greek intellectuals in Athens (Acts 17:22–31), he makes five basic points: (1) God is Creator, and Lord of heaven and earth (v. 24a); He cannot be contained in our shrines or idols (24b–25); all men and women are responsible to Him (26–30); He will judge the world (31a); He will do this by the resurrected Christ (31b).[2] Paul focuses God's creative power and rule in Christ as He is the Judge of all mankind.

You will find this "Christocentric" focus throughout the New Testament. The Gospels tell the story of Jesus' life, death, and resurrection. Acts describes how His people share His story with the world. The epistles show Christ's people how to worship and live. Revelation describes Jesus' return and eternal reign. The New Testament has only one central idea: Jesus is Lord (Acts 2:36).

To understand the focus of the Bible in Christ, think of the Scriptures as an hourglass, with movement from top to bottom.[3] Christ is the center through whom all movement flows. God's activities lead to and flow from salvation in His Son.

At the broad top of the hourglass we find God's creative activity in making His perfect world: "God saw all that He had made, and it was very good" (Gen. 1:31). But mankind chooses to rebel in pride, wanting to be "like God, knowing good and evil" (Gen. 3:5). God now begins to provide for our redemption from our sin, and the hourglass begins to narrow. God chooses Abraham as the father of the nation through which redemption will come (Gen. 12:1–3). Only a remnant of this nation is faithful to Him (Isa. 10:20–21), and the glass narrows further. Finally the glass focuses in Christ (Gal. 4:4-5).

Following Jesus' death and resurrection, the hourglass begins to broaden from Jesus to His apostles and early disciples. It then broadens further at Pentecost and the conversion of three thousand (Acts 2:41). Following the model of Acts 1:8—"you will be my witnesses in Jerusalem, and in all Judea and Samaria, and to the ends of the earth"—the church begins to grow. Samaritans are won to Christ (Acts 8), followed by Gentiles (Acts 10), and finally the gospel is carried to the world (Acts 13). When Acts ends, Paul is preaching freely in Rome, the capital of the Empire.

As the Bible predicts, the gospel will be preached to all the world and Christ will return, for "our Lord God Almighty reigns" (Rev. 19:6). Redemption in Christ will come, for Jesus is Lord. And so God's word centers in God's Son. He fulfills the Old Testament and is the focus of the New. This means that the question the Greeks asked Philip is appropriate for our study of the Bible today: "Sir, we would like to see Jesus" (John 12:21).

Check Yourself 1

1. "Christocentric" means _____.

2. Complete Matthew 5:17—"I have not come to abolish them [the Law and Prophets] but to _____ them."

3. What was the purpose of the law? (circle the best answer)

   a. To enable us to justify ourselves by keeping it

   b. To show us our need for grace and salvation

   c. To provide detailed rules for behavior

4. What was the purpose of the sacrificial system? (circle the best answer)

   a. To provide rituals to be observed for all time

   b. To enable us to justify ourselves by observing it

   c. To prepare the people to understand Jesus' sacrifice at Calvary

5. Who/what was the central theme of Peter's and Paul's preaching? _____

WHAT IS THE CENTRAL THEME OF THE BIBLE?

The Gospel of Mark introduces the ministry of Jesus Christ with the words, "The time has come. The kingdom of God is near. Repent and believe the good news!" (Mark 1:15). Matthew records Jesus' first preaching in the same way: "Repent, for the kingdom of heaven is near" (Matt. 4:17). Here we come face to face with the central theme of the Bible, expressed fully and finally in the teaching of Jesus: the Kingdom of God.

James Stewart has beautifully described the importance of this theme in God's word and the Christian faith:

> Every new idea that has ever burst upon the world has had a watchword. Always there has been some word or phrase in which the very genius of the thing has been concentrated and focused, some word or phrase to blazon on its banners when it went marching out into the world. Islam had a watchword: "God is God, and Mohammed is his prophet. The French Revolution had a watchword: "Liberty, equality, fraternity." The democratic idea had a watchword: "Government of the people, by the people, for the people.". . . Every new idea that has stirred the hearts of men has created its own watchword, something to wave like a flag, to rally the ranks and win recruits. Now the greatest idea that has ever been born upon the earth is the Christian idea. And Christianity came with a watchword, magnificent and mighty and imperial; and the watchword was: "The kingdom of God."[4]

Jesus defines the kingdom of God very simply in the model prayer: "your kingdom come, your will be done on earth as it is in heaven" (Matt. 6:10). God's kingdom comes wherever and whenever His will is done. As He is served and His will obeyed, He reigns as King.

As we will soon see, God's kingdom is central to the faith and message of the Old Testament and is the heart of Jesus' ministry and message as well.[5] And yet most Christians seem to be unfamiliar with the "kingdom of God" and its meaning. And so we need to know, what did the "kingdom" mean for the Jews? Why was it so important to Jesus? And how does it help us understand the Bible?

The Old Testament Exalts the King

Throughout the Old Testament God is constantly viewed as King. All Semitic peoples thought of their gods as kings,[6] but none more so than the Hebrews. Listen to this song of their faith:

> The Lord reigns, he is robed in majesty; the Lord is robed in majesty and is armed with strength. The world is firmly established; it cannot be moved. Your throne was established long ago; you are from all eternity (Ps. 93:1–2).

Moses and his people sang, "The Lord will reign for ever and ever" (Ex. 15:18). The prophet Balaam said of the Jews, "The Lord their God is with them; the shout of the King is among them" (Num. 23:21). At the end of his life, Moses again proclaimed God King over Israel (Deut. 33:5). The Lord claimed His rule over His people: "I am the Lord, your Holy One, Israel's Creator, your King" (Isa. 43:15). The Jewish belief in God as King was the foundation of their faith.

This rule is not confined to Israel, for the Lord's claim to kingship extends to all the earth. Hezekiah prays to God: "O Lord, God of Israel, enthroned between the cherubim, you alone are God over all the kingdoms of the earth" (2 Kings 19:15).

David declares the same: "The Lord sits enthroned over the flood; the Lord is enthroned as King forever" (Ps. 29:10). The other Psalmists join him in similar praise: "How awesome is the Lord Most High, the great King over all the earth!" (Ps. 47:2); "Say among the nations, 'The Lord reigns'" (Ps. 96:10); "The Lord reigns, let the earth be glad; let the distant shores rejoice" (Ps. 97:1). The Jewish hope was founded on the belief that their God is King of all the earth.

But here a great problem arose: while the Hebrews could affirm that God is King by faith, they seldom could by sight.

Their question was, If God rules the world now, why are His people so oppressed? Generations of persecution by foreign powers had created this crisis of faith. These struggles caused the Hebrew prophets to look to the future, predicting a time when their God would come to rule the earth in complete victory and power.

This was Isaiah's vision: "The moon will be abashed, the sun ashamed; for the Lord Almighty will reign on Mount Zion and in Jerusalem, and before its elders, gloriously" (Isa. 24:23; see 3:22, 52:7; Zeph. 3:15; and Obad. 21). Zechariah saw this clearly: "The Lord will be king over the whole earth. On that day there will be one Lord, and his name the only name" (Zech.14:9). One day, their King promises, "I will create new heavens and a new earth. . . . I will create Jerusalem to be a delight, and its people a joy. I will rejoice over Jerusalem and take delight in my people; the sound of weeping and of crying will be heard in it no more" (Isa. 65:17,18–19).

And so the Old Testament vision of the present, reigning King begins to focus on the future, coming Lord. This coming One the Jews called "Messiah," a Hebrew word meaning "anointed one." The Hebrew people saw the Messiah as the Chosen One, the representative of God, the one in whom the Lord is present and through whom He acts as King. When God rules the world, He will do so through His Messiah. For this reason "Immanuel," meaning "God with us," is an appropriate title for the coming Messiah of God (Isa.7:14).[7]

When the Messiah comes, in Him God will reign over the earth as King. Isaiah predicted of this coming one, "Of the increase of His government and peace there will be no end. He will reign on David's throne and over his kingdom, establishing and upholding it with justice and righteousness from that time on and forever" (Isa. 9:7). Isaiah 42:1 promises, "Here is my servant, whom I uphold, my chosen one in whom I delight; I will put my Spirit on him and he will bring justice to the nations." Zechariah heard the Lord promise:

> Shout and be glad, O Daughter of Zion. For I am coming, and I will live among you. . . . Many nations will be joined with the Lord in that day and will become my people. I will live among you and you will know that the Lord Almighty has sent me to you. The Lord will inherit Judah as his portion in the holy land and will again choose Jerusalem (Zech. 2:10–12).

And so by the end of the Old Testament era, many of the Jews were looking for a coming One to inaugurate the Kingdom of God on earth. This expectation prepared the way for the life, ministry, death and resurrection of God's Messiah, Jesus Christ.

JESUS THE MESSIAH FULFILLS THE KINGDOM

"Christ" is the Greek word for "Messiah." The New Testament writers referred to Jesus by this title approximately 350 times. It is abundantly clear in their writings that they and their people considered Jesus to be God's promised Messiah, the One who would usher in the kingdom. There were at least two reasons for this.

First, Jesus announced Himself to be the Messiah. One of the prophecies in Isaiah described the Messiah in this way:

> The Spirit of the Sovereign Lord is on me, because the Lord has anointed me to preach good news to the poor. He has sent me to bind up the brokenhearted, to proclaim freedom for the captives and release for the prisoners, to proclaim the year of the Lord's favor (Isa. 61:1–2).

Immediately after His wilderness temptation, Jesus went to His home synagogue in Nazareth to worship. He was handed the scroll of Isaiah to read. He found this messianic prophecy in Isaiah, read it, and said, "Today this scripture is fulfilled in your hearing" (Luke 4:21). Jesus began His public ministry by claiming clearly to be God's Messiah, the One to bring His kingdom to earth.

Accordingly, He announces at the beginning of His preaching, "the kingdom of heaven is near" (Matt. 4:17). Jesus says of himself, "If I drive out demons by the Spirit of God, then the kingdom of God has come upon you" (Matt. 12:28). He states, "The Law and the Prophets were proclaimed until John. Since that time, the good news of the kingdom of God is being preached" (Luke16:16). When the Samaritan woman at the well at Sychar said, "I know that Messiah is coming," Jesus declared, "I who speak to you am he" (John 4:25–26). Jesus claimed to be the Messiah, come to bring the kingdom to earth.

Second, Jesus fulfilled predictions about the Messiah. The Messiah would be of the seed of Abraham (Gen. 22:18), Isaac (Gen.21:12), and Jacob (Num. 24:17), of the tribe of Judah (Gen. 49:10), the family of Jesse (Isa. 11:1), and the house of David (Jer. 23:5). All this Matthew claims for Jesus as part of his effort to convince the Jews of Jesus' messiahship (Matt. 1:1-6,16).

Note these other predictions and fulfillments: the Messiah would be born at Bethlehem (Micah 5:2; Matt. 2:1). He would be virgin-born and would be called Immanuel (Isa. 7:14; Matt. 1:23). He would be preceded by a messenger (Isa. 40:3 and Mal. 3:1; fulfilled in John the Baptist, Matt. 3:1–2). His ministry would begin in Galilee (Isa. 9:1; Matt. 4:12). These and the many other Old Testament predictions which Jesus fulfilled convinced His followers that He was indeed the Messiah.

When Jesus the Messiah came to earth, He inaugurated the kingdom of God here. It was only natural that He would make this kingdom the central teaching and theme of His life and ministry.

Jesus taught His disciples to pray for the kingdom: "Your kingdom come, your will be done on earth as it is in heaven" (Matt.6:10). He taught them about the kingdom, in parables and in dialogue (see Matt. 13). He received them into the kingdom: "And I confer on you a kingdom, just as my Father conferred one on me, so that you may eat and drink at my table in my kingdom and sit on thrones, judging the twelve tribes of Israel" (Luke 22:29–30).The coming of the Spirit at Pentecost empowered the church to do the work of the kingdom. When the disciples asked Jesus, "Lord, are you at this time going to restore the kingdom to Israel?" He replied, "You will receive power when the Holy Spirit comes on you; and you will be my witnesses in Jerusalem, and in all Judea and Samaria, and to the ends of the earth" (Acts1:6,8). As the church did the will of God by the power of God, they expanded the kingdom of God across the world.

Jesus promised that one day He would return to consummate the kingdom: "When the Son of Man comes in His glory, and all the angels with Him, He will sit on His throne in heavenly glory" (Matt. 25:31). Revelation promises this glorious rule: "The kingdom of the world has become the kingdom of our Lord and of his Christ, and he will reign for ever and ever" (Rev. 11:15).[8] Because Jesus has come, the kingdom has already begun on earth. One day it will be completed by Him in glory.[9] In short, the "kingdom of God" was the central theme of Jesus' life and teaching because it is the central theme of the Bible. The Hebrews proclaimed their God King of the earth. They looked for His coming rule in Messiah. Jesus fulfilled this expectation and inaugurated God's rule on earth. The church now does the work of the kingdom in the world. One day Jesus will return to consummate God's kingdom, and He will reign forever.

THE BIBLE FINDS UNITY IN THE KINGDOM

Since the kingdom is central to the Bible, we might expect this theme to unify and organize the different parts of the Bible. When you think of the "kingdom of God" as the "hub" of Scripture and the different biblical sections as the "spokes," you can see how each relates to the others and to their central theme.

As a very general overview, let's apply this approach to the different sections of the Bible. The *creation* stories testify that God is the creating King. The *history* of the nation of Israel shows him to be the ruling King. The *law* and *wisdom* sections teach the Jews how to live in His kingdom. The *prophets* call the people to serve God as King and predict the coming of His rule in the Messiah. The *Gospels* witness to Christ as the Messiah, the present King. *Acts* tells the story of the spread of His kingdom. The *epistles* call the church to faithful life in the kingdom. And *Revelation* portrays the coming, eternal kingdom of God.

When we study the Bible in terms of the kingdom of God, we are focusing the different parts of Scripture on the theme of Scripture. The books become the Book. And this Book draws us to life in the kingdom of God. The theme of the Bible then fulfills the purpose of the Bible: "these are written that you may believe that Jesus is the Christ ["Messiah"], the Son of God, and that by believing you may have life in His name" (John 20:31). Our discussion leads us to a very practical conclusion: it helps to always relate your Bible study to the kingdom. As you study the Scriptures, ask at every turn, What does this say about the King? How does this passage help me to live faithfully in His kingdom? When you read the Bible in this way, you are applying God's word to His will for your life. This is the most fruitful way you can study the word of God.

CHECK YOURSELF 2

1. The central theme of the Bible is the _____.

2. "Messiah" means _____.

3. When Messiah comes, God will reign over the earth as _____.

4. In what ways did Jesus fulfill the role of Messiah? (circle all that apply)

    a. He announced that He was bringing in the Kingdom

    b. He fulfilled predictions about the Messiah

   c. He came as a military conqueror

   d. He taught His disciples to pray for the Kingdom

   e. He promised that one day He would return to consummate the kingdom

5. The most fruitful way you can study the word of God is to relate your Bible study to the _____.

WHAT ARE THE BOOKS OF THE BIBLE ABOUT?

Harry Emerson Fosdick was a famous American Baptist minister and professor in the first part of this century. He once said that as a young boy he wanted to read the Bible through, using the old method of reading three chapters a day and five on Sunday. However, he never succeeded because he always stalled about halfway through Jeremiah.[10] Many people have had similar problems with similar methods. Actually, reading the Bible straight through is probably the least effective way to study it because, unlike most books, it was not organized in a simple beginning-to-end manner. The Bible is not a single book, but a collection of many books.

In fact, the title "Bible" was not applied to God's word until the fourth century, when it was first used by Chrysostom, a church leader who died in A.D. 407. Early church leaders often called Scripture the "Divine Library." In 1516 the English officially designated it "Bibliotheca," meaning "sacred library." Only in recent centuries have the Scriptures commonly come to be called the "Bible."

How are these volumes organized? The Scriptures are not structured by chronological history. Rather, the Bible sets out its basic theme of God as King, each section building on the last. Within this general approach there are eight main sections, four within each Testament. Let's look briefly at these sections and their individual books in a condensed approach, so that we'll have a sense of the overall direction of the Bible.

THE OLD TESTAMENT

The Law. The Bible opens with the "Pentateuch" (meaning "five books"). This section is commonly called the Law by the Jews, because these books deal with legal requirements for holy living. Here we learn the requirements to be servants of the King. *Genesis*, meaning "origin," describes the origin of the universe, the human race, and the nation of Israel. Throughout it is the story of God the King, creating by His power and authority.

Chapters 1–11 tell the story of God's perfect creation and its fall into sin. Here we read of God's judgment in banishing Adam and Eve from Eden, destroying the world in the flood, and scattering humankind at the tower of Babel. Our need for redemption from sin is made painfully clear.

In chapter 12, God's answer to our need begins to be revealed. God calls Abram (later renamed "Abraham"), and through him founds the nation of Israel. The remainder of Genesis tells the story of Abraham's immediate descendents, Isaac, Jacob, and Joseph, known as the "patriarchs" of the nation. Here Israel is created and multiplied, so that through the nation one day God can bring the Messiah to atone for all sin.

Exodus takes its name from the Hebrews' emancipation from Egyptian slavery and departure from that nation. Here the Jewish people become a unified nation under Moses. Through him God the King leads His people across the Red Sea, gives them His laws and commandments, and directs them in His worship.

Leviticus is named for the "Levites," the Jewish tribe responsible for priestly ministry and religious life in the nation. This book describes methods by which the Hebrews are to worship their King and serve Him.

Numbers is so named because it describes two censuses, numbering the nation of Israel (chaps. 1, 26). The book further details some rules for worship and life. It tells of the people's unbelief and refusal to enter the Promised Land. It then describes their life and travels to the east of the Jordan River at the edge of the Promised Land.

Deuteronomy means "the second law." Here Moses repeats God's laws to the people shortly before they enter the Promised Land.

History. The next twelve books of the Bible are historical in nature. They span the centuries from the conquest of the Promised Land to the Jews' captivity in Babylon and the reestablishment of their nation at Jerusalem. This section takes us to the chronological end of the Old Testament period. God is the King of the nation throughout, leading His people.

Joshua takes its name from its central figure, the warrior who led the people to conquer Canaan and who later divided the land among the twelve Hebrew tribes.

Judges describes six periods of Jewish servitude to various peoples in Canaan, and the nation's deliverance through the leadership of fifteen "judges" of the people.

Ruth was a foreign woman who was eventually married to a Hebrew and who became an ancestor of Jesus (Matt. 1:5). The events of this book occur during the period of the Judges, accounting for the book's place in the biblical organization.

1 and 2 Samuel are named after Samuel, the last judge of Israel and a priest and prophet in the land. Originally there was only one book of Samuel, but the Septuagint divided it into two. While all of the events of 1 Samuel 25–31 and 2 Samuel occur after Samuel's death, he is the outstanding figure of the early sections of the book. In these books we meet Saul and David, and read of the Kingdom united under King David.

1 and 2 Kings, like 1 and 2 Samuel, were originally one book which was divided in the Septuagint. These books are named for their subject: four centuries of Hebrew kings, from David (died 930 B.C.) to Jehoiachin (in Babylon, after 561). Here we read of the Kingdom united under David and Solomon and divided after Solomon's death into Israel (called the Northern Kingdom for the ten northern tribes) and Judah (called the Southern Kingdom for the southern tribes of Judah and Benjamin). The book describes the fall of Israel to the nation Assyria in 722 B.C., and closes with the fall of Judah to Babylon which climaxed in 586 B.C.

1 and 2 Chronicles are a "miniature Old Testament." Originally one book, their narrative begins with chronologies from Adam through the twelve tribes of Israel. They then describe the reigns of Saul, David, and Solomon, followed by a history of the Southern Kingdom to its release from Babylon.

Ezra was a priest and scribe who was instrumental in leading the Jews back to Judah. Originally combined with the books of Nehemiah and Chronicles, this book tells of the release of the Jews from Babylon after Cyrus and the Persians defeated the Babylonian Empire. It describes the return of about fifty thousand Hebrews to the land of Judah, the laying of the temple foundation, and spiritual revival in the land.

Nehemiah was the governor of the rebuilding nation. He led the people to rebuild the walls of Jerusalem and helped reestablish sacred ordinances and worship in the nation.

Esther records events which occurred in the nation of Persia, chronologically between the sixth and seventh chapters of Ezra. The book is named for Queen Esther, who delivered the Jews from destruction. Noteworthy as the only book in the Bible which does not mention the name of God, Esther nonetheless testifies to the Lord's sovereignty over the foreign Persian nation.

Wisdom Literature. The next five books of the Bible are usually called "wisdom literature," as they offer precepts for religious and practical life. They show subjects of the King how to trust and please Him.

Job is named for its central, suffering figure. Job may have lived around the time of Abraham. His book, if written shortly after the events it describes, may therefore be the first biblical book to be written. The story concerns the age-old problem of suffering and the goodness of God, and it describes Job's final deliverance by his Lord.

Psalms takes its name from the Greek word for songs sung to the accompaniment of stringed instruments. It is a collection of 150 spiritual songs, poems, and prayers, and was the hymnal of the Hebrew people.

Proverbs is a collection of wise sayings dealing with every-day matters in the life of faith. Written primarily by Solomon, these principles for relationships and righteousness served the Jews as a practical guide for daily life.

Ecclesiastes is named for the Greek word which means "preacher" or "assembly." The author (traditionally thought to be Solomon) describes the vanity of life without God and our need to serve Him obediently.

Song of Solomon is so named for its author, although some call it the "Song of Songs," from its first verse. This poem is written about Solomon's love for a Shulammite girl, but it has often been interpreted in a larger sense as describing God's love for His people and/or Christ's love for His church.

The Prophets. The last section of the Old Testament contains the writings of and about the prophets. The first five of these books are often called the "major" prophets, to be distinguished from the twelve "minor" prophets which later follow. The only reason for this designation is that four of these first five books are much longer than the twelve which follow. In significance, the shorter books are no less "major" than those which precede them.

A "prophet" in the Old Testament was involved both in "fore-telling" and in "forthtelling." While the prophets did predict the future, they also preached to the needs of the present. The central thought of the prophetic books is that the Hebrew people must return to worshiping and serving God the King.

Isaiah prophesied in Judah, warning the people of the pending Babylonian captivity and calling them to return to God. The second half of this book describes life in Babylon, and exhorts the suffering people to faithfulness. The book is rich in prophecies about the coming Messiah.

Jeremiah lived from the time of King Josiah in Judah to the Babylonian captivity and sought to lead his people from their sins back to faithfulness to God.

Lamentations takes its name from the Greek verb meaning "to cry aloud," and consists of five sorrowful poems about the destruction of Jerusalem by the Babylonians. It is usually attributed to Jeremiah.

Ezekiel was a priest and prophet whose name means "God strengthens." Ezekiel spent his early years in Jersualem, and then was exiled to Babylon. Chapters 1–24 warned the Jews of the coming captivity; chapters 25–32 prophesied against foreign nations; and chapters 33– 48 offered the exiled Jews hope of a promised return to the land.

Daniel means "God is my judge." Daniel was exiled as a youth to Babylon, where he spent his life as a government official and prophet of God. He called his people to faith in the Lord and described predictive visions about the future hope of the people.

Hosea was a contemporary with Isaiah and Micah. He described the sins of the Northern Kingdom and predicted their coming judgment. The book calls the people to return to their loving God.

Joel was a prophet in Judah. His name means "Yahweh is God," and his book describes the desolation of the land due to sin and promises future deliverance.

Amos was a herdsman prophet from Judah who preached in the Northern Kingdom of Israel. He denounced the people's sins and called them back to God. His book contains predictions of future catastrophe, sermons against sin, and visions of judgment and restoration.

Obadiah means "servant of the Lord." This prophet preached of God's judgment against the nation of Edom, the descendents of Esau, Jacob's twin brother. Obadiah promised the future, final deliverance of Israel.

Jonah was a prophet from the area of Nazareth whom God called to preach against Nineveh, the wicked capital city of Assyria. His well-known story shows God's love for the entire world and the Lord's willingness to use rebellious people to accomplish His purposes.

Micah means "who is like God?" This prophet predicted future judgment for Judah, to be followed by her restoration. Micah 5:2 predicts Bethlehem as the Messiah's birthplace, and the prophet calls the people to messianic hope and faith.

Nahum means "consolation." He predicted the fall of Nineveh, an event which occurred in 612 B.C., and promised Judah's deliverance from Assyrian power.

Habakkuk means "embracer." He preached in the period just before the Babylonians began their invasions of Judah. Habakkuk showed his people that the Lord would use Babylon to punish their sins but also promised that the Babylonians would later be destroyed as well, thus vindicating the righteousness of God.

Zephaniah called Judah to repentance and revival, promising judgment for sin and blessing for righteousness.

Haggai was a contemporary of Zechariah (and of Confucius), and the first prophet to preach after the people returned from exile in Babylon. He called the nation to finish rebuilding the temple, whose completion had been delayed some fifteen years. He promised a return of God's glory when this project was done.

Zechariah means "God remembers." The prophet returned to Jerusalem from Babylon with Haggai and also called the people to complete the Temple. Zechariah made more predictions about the future Messiah than any other prophet except Isaiah.

Malachi means "my messenger." Preaching about a century after the Jews returned to Jerusalem, Malachi called his nation back to righteousness and faithfulness, thus preparing them for the Messiah to come.

The Old Testament sets the stage for the coming of God's Kingdom in His Messiah. The people are given His Law, which they continually break. This shows their need for salvation in Christ. They are given a nation, through which the Messiah will come. The wisdom literature calls this nation to faith and to worship of the King. The prophets predict judgment and offer hope in the coming One. God gave the people His spoken and written word to prepare them to receive His living word.

THE NEW TESTAMENT

The Gospels. "Gospel" means "good news." The "gospels" are so named because they offer the good news of salvation in Jesus Christ. They are not biographies as we think of them today. Instead, they record what we need to know to trust in Christ as Savior and Lord (John 20:30–31) and to live in His kingdom.

Matthew was a tax-collector who became one of Jesus' disciples. He wrote to persuade the Jews that Jesus was their long-awaited Messiah. His Gospel thus makes more use of Old Testament fulfillment than any other and records five teaching sections where Christ explains the Kingdom He brings.

Mark was a close friend of Peter; according to early tradition, he wrote his Gospel to record Peter's sermons and experiences. Mark wanted to persuade Gentile, especially Roman, readers that Jesus is the divine Son of God and thus emphasized Jesus' actions and miracles. This book is usually considered the first gospel to be written.

Luke was probably the only Gentile writer in the New Testament. He was Paul's physician and according to tradition, wrote his Gospel from Paul's experiences and preaching. He researched his book carefully, seeking to convince his Gentile readers that Jesus was their compassionate Savior.

John was Jesus' closest disciple and friend. His Gospel interprets the life of Christ, intending to persuade its reader to trust Him as Savior and Lord. John included no parables and only seven miracles of Jesus. The last half of his book focuses on Jesus' final week, explaining His death and resurrection as our only hope for eternal life.

The Gospels present Christ as Messiah, Son of God, servant and Lord. They invite their reader to enter His Kingdom by faith and to serve Him obediently.

Acts. This book is Luke's companion to his Gospel. He described the growth of Christ's church from Jerusalem to Rome, "the ends of the earth." His Gospel focused on Jesus' works; Acts centers on those of the Holy Spirit. Together these books tell of the coming and growth of the kingdom of God.

The Epistles. An "epistle" is a formal written correspondence. The New Testament contains twenty-one such letters. They are the work of six writers: Paul, Peter, James, John, Jude, and the author of Hebrews. Paul wrote thirteen epistles; Peter wrote two letters; James one; John three; and Jude one. The letters were written to individual churches, to groups of churches, and to individual persons. Paul wrote the first thirteen New Testament letters. Three of these—1 and 2 Timothy and Titus—are called the "pastorals" since they deal with pastoral issues and counsel. Paul's letters are generally arranged from longest (Romans) to shortest (Philemon). The authorship of Hebrews is still uncertain, so it is placed after Paul's letters. The last seven letters are called General Epistles, since they are addressed to the church at large.

Romans has been called the greatest book of theology ever composed. Paul's theme is justification by God's grace through faith in His Son, Jesus Christ. The letter sets out our need to be justified with God because of our sin. It then presents Christ's death as the answer to our need, calls us to holy living, explains Israel's role in God's plan, and closes with practical guidance for Christian living.

1 and 2 Corinthians were written to the church at Corinth, a notoriously sinful city. Here Paul dealt with church problems such as disunity, immorality, questions about marriage and divorce, problems with the Lord's Supper and worship.

Galatians was probably Paul's first letter. It was written to a group of churches in the region called Galatia, and deals with the Judaizing controversy about which the Jerusalem council met in Acts 15. Briefly put, the question concerned whether to require Jewish legalism for Gentile Christian converts. Paul's pointed rejection of legalism freed the church to accept God's free grace in Christ.

Ephesians was written from prison and was circulated among several churches in the general area of Ephesus (this is called a "circular" letter). The first three chapters describe the unity and spiritual blessings of the church; the last three call her members to holy living.

Philippians was also written from prison and is the most personal letter Paul wrote to any church. This church family appears to have been his favorite, and he writes to express thanks for their support. In addition he calls them to stand against Jewish legalism and to live together in unity.

Colossians is another prison letter. Paul wrote it to exalt Christ as head of the church and thus defeat the heretics in Colossae who were attempting to mislead God's people.

1 and 2 Thessalonians were written early in Paul's ministry, probably just after Galatians. They called the church at Thessalonica to continue in faithfulness to Christ in view of His future return.

1 and 2 Timothy were written toward the end of Paul's life and are addressed to Timothy, Paul's disciple and "son in the faith" in Ephesus. The letters offer advice to this young minister on practical matters of personal and pastoral ministry.

Titus is very similar in content to 1 and 2 Timothy. It was written to another young minister regarding the organization and leadership of churches, this time in Crete.

Philemon is Paul's shortest and most personal letter. Written from prison, it is addressed to Philemon, a Christian slave owner. Paul encourages him to offer mercy to Onesimus, his runaway slave who has since become a Christian. In a larger sense, the letter calls all Christians to charity and grace.

Hebrews was written to exalt Jesus as our great High Priest. The letter emphasizes Christ's superiority and shows how He fulfills Old Testament Judaism as the Son of God. On this basis the writer encouraged his readers to steadfast faithfulness in spite of growing persecution.

James was probably written by Jesus' half-brother, the recognized leader of the church at Jerusalem. The letter calls its readers to a practical, daily lifestyle of dedicated discipleship.

1 and 2 Peter were probably written by the apostle shortly before his death at the hands of Nero in Rome in A.D. 64. Here he called his people to faithfulness in the face of suffering and persecution, and to orthodox belief in spite of growing heresy.

1, 2, and 3 John were probably written toward the end of the first century A.D. by John the apostle. He wrote as a pastor to encourage his people to faith, joy, and assurance in Christ. John called upon the church to love one another as their witness to the world.

Jude was probably written by another of Jesus' half-brothers. It warns the church about false teachers, predicts their judgment, and calls the people to "contend for the faith" (v. 3).

Revelation. This last book of the Bible takes its title from the Greek word which means "unveiling." Here Jesus is unveiled before the apostle John and his readers in all His heavenly glory and power. Christ promises His suffering people that He is with them and will one day return in judgment and victory.

Before you begin to study any part of the Bible, it helps to have clearly in mind that book's general idea and purpose. Such an overview can help you prepare for more effective study of God's word.

CHECK YOURSELF 3

1. T/F: Reading the Bible straight through is usually a very effective way to study God's word.

2. T/F: Only in recent centuries have the Scriptures commonly been called the "Bible."

3. "Pentateuch" means _____.

4. The four divisions of the Old Testament are:

    a. _____

    b. _____

    c. _____

    d. _____

5. The four divisions of the New Testament are:

    a. _____

    b. _____

    c. _____

    d. _____

How Do the Books of the Bible Relate to Each Other?

We tend to read books in a "linear" fashion, treating them as one continuous story from beginning to end. As we have seen, the Bible is not organized in this way. It may be helpful, therefore, to close this chapter with a brief chronological and thematic arrangement of the Scriptures. While the question of biblical chronology remains a much-debated subject among scholars, we can at least trace broad historical lines. The following charts will help you see the biblical books in historical perspective.

The Old Testament[11]

The chronology given below depends on commonly accepted dates for events and books. This overview is intended as a general survey, since discussing debates about dates and arrangements would be beyond the scope of our study.

Events	Biblical Books
1. *Beginnings (undated)*	*Genesis 1–11*
Creation of the world	
Adam and Eve	
Cain and Abel	
Cain's line Seth's line	
Noah and the flood	
Ham, Shem and Japheth (humankind divided by nations)	
The Tower of Babel (humankind divided by languages)	
2. *The Patriarchs (approx. 1900–1300 B.C.)*	*Genesis 12–50*
Abram (Abraham) and Sarai (Sarah)	*Job?*
Isaac	
Jacob (Israel)	
The Sons of Israel	
Settlement of Jacob's family in Egypt	
Four hundred years of captivity by the Egyptians	
3. *Exodus and the wilderness (1300-1250 B.C.)*	*Exodus*
Moses and the exodus from Egypt	*Numbers*
The giving of the Law at Sinai	*Deuteronomy*
The nation's refusal to enter the Promised Land	*Joshua*

Forty years of wilderness wanderings
Joshua's leadership and the conquest of the Land

4. *The tribal confederacy (1250–1020 B.C.)*   *Judges*
   Period of the fifteen judges   *Ruth*

5. *The united kingdom (1020-922 B.C.)*   *1 and 2 Samuel*
   Saul (1020–1000 B.C.)   *1 and 2 Kings*
   David (1000–961 B.C.)   *Psalms*
   Solomon (961–922 B.C.)   *Proverbs*
                                                   Song of Solomon
                                                       Ecclesiastes
                                                1 and 2 Chronicles

6. *The divided kingdom: Israel and Judah*
   Israel—the northern kingdom (922–722 B.C.)   *Joel (ca. 830)*
   nine royal lines, nineteen kings   *Amos (ca. 750)*
                                                  Hosea (ca. 710)
   Judah—the southern kingdom (922–586 B.C.)   *Jonah (ca. 760)*
   David's royal line, twenty kings   *Isaiah (ca. 740)*
                                                  Micah (ca. 700)
                                              Zephaniah (ca. 625)
                                                 Nahum (ca. 610)
                                              Habakkuk (ca. 610)
                                                 Obadiah (586 ?)
                                  Jeremiah/Lamentations (585)

7. *The exile to Babylon (586–538 B.C.)*   *Ezekiel (ca. 570)*
                                                   Daniel (ca. 540)

8. *The return to Jerusalem (538 B.C.)*   *Esther*
   Cyrus, king of Persia,
      conquers Babylon (539–538)
   First exiles return with Zerubbabel (537)
                                                    Haggai (ca. 520)
                                                 Zechariah (ca. 520)
   The Temple is rebuilt and
      dedicated (516)
   The return under the leadership
      of Nehemiah (464–423)   *Nehemiah*
                                                 Malachi (ca. 420)
   The return led by Ezra (404)   *Ezra*

The close of the Old Testament period (ca. 400)

THE NEW TESTAMENT

As with the Old Testament, the question of the chronological arrangement of the New Testament is a subject that scholars debate today. We'll suggest a simple linear arrangement without getting involved in this larger discussion.

1. *The Gospels*
   Mark (45–50's, assuming his is the first to be written)
   Luke (60–61?)
   Matthew (60's; some believe that his was the first written)
   John (90's)

2. *Acts (ca. 61)*

3. *Epistles—by grouping, in approximate order of composition*

   Paul's early letters (ca. 49–58):
   Galatians
   1 Thessalonians
   2 Thessalonians
   1 Corinthians
   2 Corinthians
   Romans

   Prison epistles (probably written from prison in Rome, ca. 61):
   Philemon
   Colossians
   Ephesians
   Philippians

   Pastoral letters (ca. 63– 66):
   1 Timothy
   Titus
   2 Timothy
   Hebrews (ca. 64– 68)

   General epistles: James (ca. 45–50)
   1, 2 Peter (ca. 63– 66)
   Jude (ca. 70–80) 1, 2, 3 John (ca. 90)

4. Revelation (ca. 90s)

CONCLUSION

In this chapter we have discussed some important aspects of the Bible which are often overlooked. Christ is the *central figure* of the Bible. When we study God's word to learn more about Him, we fulfill Scripture's purpose (John 20:31). The kingdom of God is the central theme of the Bible. Therefore, we read the Scriptures to learn how to live in the kingdom as God's child and servant. In addition, it is helpful to study any passage of God's word with the themes of the individual book and the entire Bible in mind. In this way, we can relate the parts to the whole. The entire counsel of the Scriptures will come into focus. And we will get more from God's word.

ANSWERS

CHECK YOURSELF 1

1. Christ is central   2. fulfill   3.b   4.c   5. Jesus Christ

CHECK YOURSELF 2

1. Kingdom of God   2. anointed one   3. King   4. a, b, d, e
5. kingdom

CHECK YOURSELF 3

1. F   2. T   3. five books   4. a: law; b: history; c: wisdom;
d: prophets   5. a: Gospels; b: Acts; c: epistles; d: Revelation

5

WHAT ARE THE
BEST TOOLS?

Translations and Guides to God's Word

W illiam Tyndale lived over four hundred years ago. In his day, the church would allow only its leaders to read and interpret the Bible. It also refused to let the Scriptures be translated from Latin into the language of the people. God gave Tyndale a deep desire to give people a Bible they could read for themselves, but he was unable to convince the church to do this work. He therefore began the enormous task of translating the Bible into English himself.

Tyndale worked feverishly from dawn to dusk, six days a week, for eleven years. He taught himself Hebrew in order to translate the Old Testament. All during this time the church opposed his work and even placed a bounty on his head. He finally completed the New Testament in 1525. Since printing had been invented recently, this became the first English New Testament to be printed and distributed widely. Tragically, in 1536 he was captured and executed before he could finish the Old Testament. Courageous to the end, as he stood before the gallows he prayed, "Lord, open the eyes of the King of England."

Within three years God answered his prayer, for in 1539 King Henry VIII instructed all publishers to permit "the free and liberal use of the Bible in our native tongue." And in 1611 the authorized version of King James I was published—the King James Version still in use today.

Here's the irony: the King James Version is 90 percent the work of William Tyndale. The king's scholars employed almost entirely Tyndale's censored work of a century earlier. God used the sacrifice of this man to give us a Bible we can still read and understand today. In fact, the King James Version remains the most popular Bible translation to this day. If you're like most people, your first copy of God's word came mostly from the pen of William Tyndale.

As a young man Tyndale had vowed that he would make it possible for even a plowboy to know the Bible. God fulfilled Tyndale's desire to help His people read and understand the Scriptures. And the Lord continues to use this kind of work today.

In this chapter we will look at the work of modern Tyndales. Where did today's translations of the Bible come from? Why are there so many? Which one is right for you? What commentaries and other study helps will help you most? These are important questions for all who want to unlock God's word for themselves.

The Story of the English Bible

As we saw in the first chapter, the Bible originally was written in Hebrew, Aramaic, and Greek. Since most people are unfamiliar with these languages, we must rely on a Bible which has been translated into English. For this reason a good Bible translation is your most essential tool for understanding God's word.

Fortunately, there are scores of such translations available today. In fact, the Bible is the most translated book in the world. Where did our English versions of the Bible come from?

THE FIRST TRANSLATIONS

Long before Tyndale published his English Bible, scholars were working to give their people a Bible they could read. The first effort of this kind was made by seventy-two Jewish scholars who translated the Hebrew Old Testament into Greek, the common language of their day. This translation of the Old Testament is called the Septuagint, for the "seventy" who did its work. (It is sometimes abbreviated "LXX," the Roman numeral for seventy.) This version was completed by 100 B.C.

It is interesting to know that this Greek Old Testament was the popular Bible of Jesus' day. When the New Testament writers quote the Old Testament, they usually quote the Septuagint. Most versions today still mainly follow its order of the Old Testament books.

One other early translation deserves our attention: the Latin Vulgate. In the fourth century, a scholar in the Catholic Church named Jerome wanted to give people a Bible in Latin, since this had become the common language of the day. So he made this "common" translation. In fact the name of his version—the "Vulgate"—stands for the "vulgar" or "common" Latin of the day. It is ironic that long after Latin passed from the scene as a common language, the church still insisted that this "common" Bible be used. Later, the first attempts to give people a Bible in "common" English were based on Jerome's "common" Latin Bible.

THE BIBLE INTO ENGLISH[1]

The story of the English Bible begins with the introduction of Christianity into Great Britain, probably around the third-century A.D. The first British Christians made rough translations of the Bible into their Anglo-Saxon language, completing the Gospels and some of the Old Testament by the ninth-century.

Versions of other parts of the Bible were made up to the fourteenth-century. Then John Wycliffe (died 1384) and his followers made the first effort to translate the entire Bible into the people's language.

Wycliffe was a scholar at Oxford. It was his heartfelt belief that the people should have a Bible they could read for themselves. He began this work and his followers completed it. However, the official church rejected his work, and him with it.

In fact, his remains were exhumed after his death and burned along with his books. But Wycliffe's movement to make the Bible available to everyone could not be stopped. His version, known as the Wycliffe Bible, was the first complete Bible in English.

It was translated from poor manuscripts, however, and was never widely available. The work of making a better translation and distributing it effectively was accomplished later by William Tyndale.

Tyndale was a notable scholar himself, educated at Oxford and later at Cambridge. Determined to make a Bible for the people, he worked at the project from 1523 until his death. Official reaction to his work was hostile—the seaports were watched to check imports, many copies were burned, and Tyndale himself was executed in 1536. Despite these efforts, however, Tyndale's English Bible soon gained wide popularity and set the stage for many similar efforts to come.

In 1535 Miles Coverdale published the first complete printed English Bible. The first English Bible approved by the king was the Matthews Bible in 1537, a version which relied heavily on the Tyndale and Coverdale Bibles. The Taverner Bible of 1539 was the first version to be printed completely in England. The Great Bible of 1539 became the first English Bible authorized by the king for use in the churches.

The most notable effort between Tyndale and the King James Version was the Geneva Bible of 1557. It employed the best scholarship of any English Bible to that point. This Bible was also the first version in English to include verse divisions. It featured maps, tables, chapter summaries, and section titles as well. As a result, the Geneva Bible became the household Bible of English-speaking Protestants. It was the Bible of Shakespeare, John Bunyan, and the pilgrims.

Following the Geneva Bible came the second version authorized by the king for church use: the Bishops Bible of 1568. This became the seventh English Bible to appear in Britain in less than five decades.

THE KING JAMES VERSION

In the space of fifty years the English people found themselves with an unfamiliar problem: instead of having no Bible in their language, they had to choose from at least seven different versions! Which one of these should the church read from in worship? Which was best for personal study? To solve this problem, King James I of England convened a committee of fifty scholars in July of 1604. Their charge was to make a new English translation of the Bible from the original languages, giving the people a version everyone could use. Seven years later they completed their task. The famous King James Version the most popular English Bible of all time, was the result. From 1611 through the nineteenth-century, this was the Bible of English-speaking Protestants everywhere.

CHECK YOURSELF I

1. Match the name on the left with the description on the right:

    ____ William Tyndale   a. The first person to try to translate the complete Bible into English

    ____ The Septuagint   b. Translated in 1611, now the most popular English Bible in history

    ____ The Vulgate   c. Published the first New Testament in English

    ____ John Wycliffe   d. Jerome's translation of the Bible into Latin

    ____ The Geneva Bible   e. The first English Bible to include verse divisions, maps, tables, chapter summaries, and section titles; the Bible of Shakespeare, Bunyan, and the pilgrims

    ____ The King James Version   f. Translation of the Old Testament into Greek; the popular Bible of Jesus' day

WHY SO MANY VERSIONS?

For nearly three hundred years, the King James Version held first place in popularity. However, this situation has changed greatly in the last century. The movement toward contemporary versions began with the Revised Version in England in 1885 and its American counterpart, the American Standard Version of 1901.

From then to today a host of modern Bible versions have become popular. Leading a Bible study in my first church staff ministry, I happened to use a translation other than the King James. After one session, a deacon stopped me in the hall. "Why aren't you using the King James?" he demanded. "If it was good enough for Peter and Paul, it's good enough for you!" Perhaps he thought Peter and Paul lived to 1611, the year the King James Version was published, or maybe he believed King James was one of the original disciples. However mistaken his knowledge of history, his feelings were real— and popular. Many Christians today want to know, What's wrong with the King James? Why are there so many of these new versions?

Making new translations of the Bible may seem to be a recent development, but in fact it is not. Nearly as long as there has been a Bible, there have been changes in manuscript study, scholarship, archaeology, and language. Barely one hundred years after the New Testament was written, Origen of Alexandria was devoting years of his life to gathering and studying the versions of the Bible which existed even then. As we have seen, the King James Version itself is based on other translations and versions of God's word.

The King James is still the most popular version. Many preachers use it, and Christians find God in its pages. However, four factors have contributed to the important role modern translations also play in today's church.

NEW DISCOVERIES IN BIBLICAL MANUSCRIPTS

When the King James translators did their work, they were limited to the manuscripts available to them. Of these, they wisely chose to translate those manuscripts which were oldest and thus closest to the original writings of the Bible. However, their New Testament manuscripts were still more than a thousand years removed from the originals. This means that they had accumulated the mistakes of over a thousand years of copying by hand. While few of these mistakes make any difference in important doctrines, many of them do affect the meaning of certain texts.

In recent centuries better manuscripts have been discovered—entire New Testaments six hundred years older than those available to the King James translators, as well as fragments which are nine hundred years older. Old Testament manuscript discoveries have been no less spectacular. The "Dead Sea Scrolls," Old Testament manuscripts found in 1947 in caves near the Dead Sea, are dated from 100 B.C. to A.D. 70, a thousand years older than those available to the King James scholars. Since these newly discovered manuscripts of the Old and New Testaments are much closer in age to the originals, they are a much better basis for translating the Bible. For this reason, biblical scholars Gordon Fee and Douglas Stuart go so far as to say, "This [fact of better manuscripts] is why for study *you should use almost any modern translation rather than the KJV* (emphasis theirs).[2] We want our English Bible to translate as closely as possible to what the authors actually wrote in their own languages. Modern versions are based on the oldest and best copies available of these originals.

IMPROVEMENTS IN SCHOLARSHIP

Bible translations are the work of men and women who have devoted their lives to studying the original biblical languages. As with any profession, these scholars continue to improve their techniques and skills. This century has witnessed many advances in understanding the grammar and language of the original Bible. As scholars learn more about how to translate the first languages of the Scripture, they will continue to revise and update their versions.

This work of revision is not new. In fact, the process affected even the King James Version. Not many people know that this version underwent five such revisions. The 1611 version was revised in 1613, with over three hundred changes made from the original edition. Further revisions were made in 1629 and 1638. In 1653 the Parliament passed a bill permitting further revision when necessary, although nothing more was changed until 1762. In 1769 yet another revision was done and this edition of the King James is the version with which we are familiar.

As biblical scholarship continues to improve, undoubtedly still more Bible revisions and translations will result. We should be grateful for the expertise of scholars who continually study and work to help us read and understand what God inspired.

FINDINGS IN ARCHAEOLOGY

One of the most fascinating areas of advance in biblical research has been in archaeology. As this science unearths records from long-past eras, it gives us windows into history. Many of these discoveries clarify the Bible itself.

For instance, in Hosea 3:2 we find a word which occurs nowhere else in the Old Testament. The word is "lethech," and is used for a particular measure of barley. Since it appears nowhere else, some scholars felt the manuscripts were in error. In two recently discovered texts, however, the word is used as it was in Hosea, to describe a unit of dry measure. Recent archaeology helped us translate this text.

Another example comes from Proverbs 26:23, where the words "kesef sigim" are found. The KJV translates this "silver dross": "Burning lips and a wicked heart are like a potsherd covered with silver dross." But a recently discovered Ugaritic text contains the word "kesapsigim," meaning "like glaze." Undoubtedly this is the word found in Proverbs. The RSV therefore translates the verse, "Like glaze covering an earthen vessel are smooth lips with an evil heart."[3] As new discoveries are made in archaeology, they will continue to affect our understanding of the Bible. Improved translations will be the result.

CHANGES IN THE ENGLISH LANGUAGE

In the King James translation of Psalm 119:147 we read, "I prevented the dawn of the morning." Is this some miracle of nature, similar to Joshua's preventing the movement of the sun and moon (Josh. 10:12–13)? Can the dawn be "prevented"?

Yes, if you know that in the days when the King James Version was translated, "prevent" meant "precede." If you get up before sunrise, you "prevent" the dawn. This is just one example of changes in the English language from 1611 to today. These changes are perhaps the most critical reason why modern versions of the Bible are so important for studying the Scriptures today.

The changes in English from 1611 to today fall into three categories. First, there are words in the KJV which are archaic today but still understandable. Personal pronouns like "thee" and "thou" are examples. You would never use these words, but you can still follow their meaning.

Second, there are words and phrases which are obsolete and no longer understandable to the average reader. In Acts 5 we read about the crowd in Jerusalem, "And of the rest durst no man join himself to them" (v. 13). Few readers would know the meaning of "durst" today.

Third and most important, there are many words in the King James which we still use today but which have a very different meaning for us than they held for the translators in 1611. These words were once accurate translations of the Hebrew or Greek, but their English meaning has changed and they are now misleading.

In the KJV "let" means "hinder," "allow" means "approve," "conversation" means "conduct of life," "comprehend" means "overcome," and "ghost" means "spirit." There are more than three hundred such words in the KJV.

Let's look at some other examples. In 1611 "charity" meant "love." Anyone who has done volunteer work knows that "Charity suffereth long, and is kind" (1 Cor. 13:4, KJV), but this is clearly not the meaning of this verse today. When Hebrews 13:5 commands us, "Let your conversation be without covetousness" (KJV), it seems we're told not to ask for things we shouldn't have. But the author actually means that we're not to live our lives covetously.

In Luke 19 we find the famous story of Zacchaeus, the tiny tax collector who climbed the sycamore tree to see Jesus. Do you know why he had to climb the tree? Verse 3 in the KJV says, "And he sought to see Jesus who he was; and could not for the press, because he was little of stature." The verse creates for us the humorous image of reporters on the scene, cameras and notepads in hand, preventing Zacchaeus from seeing Jesus. Obviously this was not the case— "press" simply meant "crowd" in 1611. This kind of confusion will only get worse as the English language continues to change.

The translators of the Revised Standard Version of 1952 were right when they said, "It not only does the King James translators no honor, but it is quite unfair to them and to the truth which they understood and expressed, to retain these words which now convey meanings they did not intend."[4] This is why R.C. Sproul concludes, "If we are looking for a beautiful translation, then the King James Version is the one. But, if we are interested in accuracy and purity of biblical translation, we must go beyond the King James Bible."[5] We must have translations of God's word which say today what He said originally.

Notice that these versions are themselves also subject to revision. Alongside the New English Bible of 1970 we now have its revision, the Revised English Bible of 1989. The Revised Standard Version of 1952 has now been reworked as the New Revised Standard Version of 1990. As language changes, so will our translations of God's unchanging truth. These different versions of the Bible are part of God's work to get His word to us.

CHECK YOURSELF 2

Choose the best answer to complete the sentence.

We have new versions of the Bible today because of:

1. New discoveries in biblical _____

2. Improvements in _____

3. Findings in _____

4. Changes in the (circle the best answer below):

    a. archaeology

    b. English language

    c. manuscripts

    d. scholarship

5. The King James Version used today is the version of:

    a. 1611   b. 1613   c. 1762   d. 1769

HOW TO CHOOSE YOUR VERSION

Which of today's translations is right for you? Finding a version you can understand and trust is important to your study of the Bible. In fact, using the best translations is the first and most important step to better Bible study. But how can you know which to choose?

The sheer number of options can be intimidating. I went to a local Christian bookstore the other day and found over thirty different translations of the Bible. That doesn't count all the styles—large print, pocket size, ultra thin—and different kinds of study Bibles on the shelf. In reading them, it's clear that all versions are not the same. Take a minute to look over these different versions of the same text, John 1:11–13.

(KJV) He came unto his own, and his own received him not. But as many as received him, to them gave he power to become the sons of God, even to them that believe on his name: Which were born, not of blood, nor of the will of the flesh, nor of the will of man, but of God.

(Living Bible) Even in his own land and among his own people, the Jews, he was not accepted. Only a few would welcome and receive him. But to all who received him, he gave the right to become children of God. All they needed to do was to trust him to save them. All those who believe this are reborn!—not a physical rebirth resulting from human passion or plan—but from the will of God.

(Revised English Bible) He came to his own, and his own people would not accept him. But to all who did accept him, to those who put their trust in him, he gave the right to become children of God, born not of human stock, by the physical desire of a human father, but of God.

(New International Version) He came to that which was his own, but his own did not receive him. Yet to all who received him, to those who believed in his name, he gave the right to become the children of God—children born not of natural descent, nor of human decision or a husband's will, but born of God.

Now, how can you decide which of these versions is best for you?

KNOW THE DIFFERENT METHODS OF BIBLE TRANSLATION[6]

There are three basic ways that scholars translate the Bible. These different approaches account for the differences in the versions available today. When you know which method best meets your needs, you'll be prepared to pick the right version for you.

The Literal Approach. The most common theory until recent times has been the "literal" approach. The most popular examples of this approach today are the King James Version and the New American Standard Version of 1960.

Those who use this approach try to keep as close as possible to the exact words and phrasings in the original biblical language. As a result, these versions help you to know the original words and phrases of the biblical author, which is often very helpful in Bible study. However, there are times when this exact equivalent may not make the best sense in English today.

There's a Greek phrase in Romans 12:20 which is literally translated, "coals of fire." This is the translation of the King James Version. But no one talks this way today. For this reason the New International Version translates the phrase "burning coals," and the New English Bible renders it "live coals."

Another, more serious example is 1 John 3:9. The KJV renders the literal words of the Greek: "Whosoever is born of God doth not commit sin." This sentence has led many Christians in times of sin to question their salvation. And it is in fact the literal statement which John made. But this is not what John meant to say. There is a way the Greek language could be used to convey a different sense with these literal words, so that they actually mean: "Whosoever is born of God does not *continue* to sin." This comes close to the NIV's translation: "No one who is born of God will continue to sin."

The "literal" translations are helpful in giving us the exact words of the original author. If you want this kind of information, a literal translation is what you need. But remember, such versions sometimes confuse the author's meaning for us today.

For this reason most people should not choose a literal translation as their primary Bible for personal study. You should, however, consult a literal translation when studying a passage to get a sense of the exact words of the original.

The "Free" Approach. At the other end of the spectrum is the "free" or "paraphrasing" theory. Those who use this approach translate the *ideas* from the original language to ours, with less concern about the actual words themselves. The most popular example of this approach is the Living Bible of 1972.

Paraphrasing helps you to read the Bible easily because it smooths out confusing phrases and unfamiliar words. This kind of version is also helpful for those who have little religious background. These reasons have made paraphrased Bibles very popular in recent years.

The problem with this approach is that you sometimes lose the original sense of the text you're reading. The words can be so updated that they lose the author's intended meaning. For example, the Living Bible translates 1 Cor. 12:1: "And now, brothers, I want to write about the special abilities the Holy Spirit gives to each of you, for I don't want any misunderstanding about them." *No* other version of which I am aware translates the Greek word here as "special abilities." The Greek wording which Paul used means "spiritual gifts." For this reason the NIV says, "Now about spiritual gifts, brothers, I do not want you to be ignorant." Other versions use much the same language.

Granted, many readers today may not understand what "spiritual gifts" are, especially if they have little religious background. But to make this phrase "special abilities" completely obscures Paul's meaning. So although the Living Bible finishes the verse, "I don't want any misunderstanding about them," it may actually add to the confusion Paul wanted to avoid.

Free translations can help you read the Bible more easily. If you are just beginning personal Bible study or otherwise need a basic translation, this may be your approach. For most people, however, the free versions are not the best primary Bible for study.

The "Dynamic Equivalence" Approach. The third approach to translating the Bible is called the "dynamic equivalence" theory. Those who follow this approach will translate the original words as exactly as they can, unless this exact rendering obscures the author's intended meaning. At these times the translators will use other words to convey more precisely the idea of the original. As a result the "dynamic equivalence" approach is a combination of the "literal" and the "free," and the best of both. The New International Version is the most popular example of this approach.

Below is a chart which places today's more popular versions along an approximate line from "literal" to "free":[7]

Literal		Dynamic Equivalence		Free	
KJV	NRSV	NIV	GNB	Phillips	LB
NKJV		NAB	JB		CP
NASB			REB		
			CEB		

USE THE BEST OF ALL THREE APPROACHES

Of all these theories and translations, which one should you use? Actually, the best approach is to use at least one version from each of the three types of translations. For a literal translation, the New American Standard is probably best. It gives you the words of the original as literally as the King James, but uses better manuscripts and avoids outdated English words. For a "free" translation, the Phillips would work well.

For a good reading Bible I recommend the Revised English Bible; in fact, this "free" translation is my personal favorite. For your primary study version the New International Version is likely the best you will find. It was produced by a committee of outstanding scholars, and combines faithfulness to the literal text with wise updating where needed. Fee and Stuart offer the same advice: "We would venture to suggest that the NIV is as good a translation as you will get."[8]

A suggested approach to Bible versions would be to study from the NIV, comparing its translation with that of the NASB and the Revised English or Phillips versions. As no one version is always the best in translating any language into English, so with the Bible. Try using these different versions together. You'll find that they help you better understand what God said. And that is the point of all translations of His word.

A WORD OF PERSPECTIVE

We have been looking together at one of the more controversial subjects in Bible study today. There are those who have the heartfelt conviction that the King James Version is the only proper Bible to study. On the other hand, some insist that you should study almost anything *but* the King James. And others are adamant that their personal preference should be yours as well.

In this confusing area, it may help to hear William Tyndale's word about Bible versions. As you'll remember, he gave us our first printed English New Testament nearly a century before the King James Version was published. In the prologue to his work he stated clearly the purpose of his translation and the need for others to revise his work:

As concerning all I have translated or otherwise written, I beseech all men to read it for that purpose I wrote it: even to bring them to the knowledge of the scripture. And as far as the scripture approveth [my translation], so far to allow it, and if in any place the word of God disallow it, there to refuse it, as I do before our saviour Christ and his congregation. And where they find faults, let them show it me, if they be nigh, or write to me, if they be far off: or write openly against it and improve it, and I promise them, if I shall perceive that their reasons conclude I will confess mine ignorance openly.[9]

As Tyndale would agree, translating the Scriptures remains a critical and essential task today. We are indebted to those who render this service to God and his people.

CHECK YOURSELF 3

1. Match the name on the left with the description on the right:

____	Literal approach	a.	Translates the ideas of the author, with less concern for the actual words he used
____	Free approach	b.	Translates exactly unless other words would better convey the author's intended meaning
____	Dynamic Equivalence approach	c.	Tries to convey the exact words and phrasings in the original biblical language

2. The best approach to using Bible translations is:

   a. The literal approach

   b. The free approach

   c. The dynamic equivalence approach

   d. Using one version from each type

3. According to William Tyndale, we should:

   a. Oppose the creating of new versions

b. Support and use the continuing work of Bible translators

c. Settle on one version and reject the rest

What Other Study Tools Are Best?

Good translations are the the most important tools for your Bible study, but not the only ones you need. Scholars have produced a wide variety of other tools also, all designed to help you get more from God's word.[10]

Commentaries

Let's begin with one of the most popular tools: commentaries.

What is a commentary? A commentary may be defined as a scholarly work which is intended to help you better understand the Bible. It can be one volume covering the entire Bible, or a large set of volumes on the individual biblical books. Usually a commentary will introduce you to the book you are studying, answering questions such as: Who was the author? When, where and why did he write? To whom? What is the book about? The writer then usually tries to explain the book verse by verse.

A commentary often includes a set of maps, a glossary of biblical words, and introductory articles such as "The History of Israel," "The Life of Jesus," "The Formation of the Bible," "Doctrines of the Old and New Testaments," "The Life of Paul," and so on. For example, *The Interpreter's Bible,* written by 150 scholars from England and America, is a twelve-volume set; its first volume contains 436 pages of articles introducing the Bible, followed by 25 pages of introduction to the Book of Genesis and 364 pages of commentary on Genesis itself.

A good commentary supplies three things. It helps you to know the historical and cultural practices of the text. It helps clarify and explain the verses themselves. And it discusses difficult passages, showing you their possible meanings.

The Dangers of Commentaries. A good commentary can be an indispensable friend in your Bible study. However, a commentary can also hinder your study if you depend upon it too much. Remember, every commentary writer is a fallible person who is giving you his or her opinions. No commentary is guaranteed reliable, for no scholar is perfect.

For this reason you should study the text for yourself before consulting any commentary or other study aid. Chapter 7 will tell you more about methods of personal Bible study. First see what God says to you in His word, and then see what others say as well.

Evaluating Commentaries. Once you know how and why to consult a commentary, which one(s) should you use? There are seven factors to consider.[11]

(1) The commentary should devote most of its space to explaining the biblical text. (This is called an "exegetical" commentary.) Many popular commentaries devote more space to the writer's applications than to the biblical text itself. (These are called "homiletical" or "devotional" commentaries.) They will offer insights into ways to preach or apply the passage, but do not help as much with the actual words of the text. For this reason, the best commentaries for study purposes are the exegetical. You want a commentary to guide you to better understand the Bible itself.

(2) The author should work with the biblical languages rather than depending on English translations. You want the writer to be familiar with the text as it was originally written.

(3) When a text has more than one possible meaning, the writer should discuss all the possibilities. He or she should evaluate them and then give reasons for these opinions. While many commentaries give only one approach to every text and question, you want a commentary to explain all the options so you can decide for yourself. This is perhaps the most important consideration in choosing a commentary.

(4) The writer should discuss questions about the original text and its wording where they affect the meaning of the passage. If differences in the ancient manuscripts are important to the study of the passage, you need to know it.

(5) The author should give you the historical background of the text where this is helpful.

(6) The author should tell you about other studies of the text or subject so you can do further work yourself.

(7) The writer should introduce the biblical book so that you know about its author, his times and readers, and his basic themes.

Are there some specific commentaries to suggest? For most readers, the Tyndale series on the Old Testament is usually helpful. While commentaries on every Old Testament book have not yet been published in this series, those already available are well worth consulting. The *New International Commentary* is gaining popularity every year. Other popular sets include *The Bible Speaks Today*, the *Bible Student's Commentary*, the *Communicator's Commentary*, the *Expositor's Bible Commentary*, and the *Interpreter's Bible*.[12]

For the New Testament, the most popular set remains *Barclay's Daily Study Bible* series. While I sometimes disagree with Dr. Barclay's theological conclusions, I am always helped by his excellent historical insights. The Tyndale New Testament series is also very helpful. The old *American Commentary* series on the New Testament contains some classic individual volumes, especially its commentary on Matthew. The *New American Commentary* while in the early stages of publication, is already winning positive reviews by scholars. And the *New International Commentary on the New Testament* continues to grow in popularity as well.

In addition, don't overlook volumes which are not part of a set. These individual commentaries on a biblical book are often among the best treatments of that subject. And don't neglect the more technical volumes which are intended for use by scholars, such as the *International Critical Commentary*. Any commentary which deals with the seven issues detailed above will help you get more from the Scriptures.

A COMMENTARY CHECKLIST

- Does the commentary explain the text thoroughly?

- Does the writer use the original languages?

- Does he or she give all the options for interpreting the passage?

- Does the author discuss the original text and its wording?

- Does the writer provide historical background to the text?

- Does the author give you sources for further study?

- Does the commentary introduce the biblical book thoroughly?

Remember that a commentary is a means to an end. If it helps guide you in meeting God in His word, it has accomplished its purpose. As an elderly lady said to one of my seminary faculty colleagues following his Sunday morning sermon, "The Bible sure throws a lot of light on those commentaries."

OTHER STUDY TOOLS

A number of other reference guides will also help you to study the Bible for yourself. Let's look briefly at some of them.

Concordances. A concordance is a book which lists alphabetically the words of the Bible, with a list of verses in which the word is found. This is one of the most helpful tools you can own.

The word "concordance" means "of the same heart." The first one is said to have been made in Latin by a Cardinal Hugo, who died in 1262. Five hundred monks helped him arrange the 773,000 words of the Bible. The first English concordance was done by John Merbecke in the reign of Edward the Sixth (1547–53).

If you need to find a verse but can only remember a few of its words, a concordance is what you need. This tool can also help you trace a word through the Bible. For instance, if you need to know everything the Bible says about the "Passover," look this word up and you will find every verse which uses it.

A limited concordance is found in the back of most Bibles. These will list most of the references to the more common biblical words. To get a complete listing of all words and verses you need a large-volume concordance such as Strong's or Young's.

Dictionaries. A Bible dictionary defines the words which appear in the Bible. It gives their background and use in the Scriptures, and shows their historical context as well. In studying a particular word or concept, a Bible dictionary can be invaluable.

For instance, the *Holman Bible Dictionary* article on "love" defines the word and then describes its use in the Old Testament, the teachings of Jesus, the teachings of Paul, and the writings of John. The article then closes with a discussion of the question of love and judgment.[13] Such help will greatly deepen your knowledge of the Scriptures and their meaning today.

Most study Bibles include a small dictionary. For more help, you should buy a good Bible dictionary for your personal study library.

Encyclopedias. A Bible encyclopedia is a kind of expanded dictionary. It treats not only biblical words but also concepts, themes, and events. For instance, if you look up "Bible" in the *International Standard Bible Encyclopedia* you will find eleven pages treating names for the Bible, languages, divisions, literary origins and canonicity, inspiration, and chapters and verses.[14]

The more you need to know about a word or concept, the more you will want to consult a Bible encyclopedia. There are several one-volume encyclopedias available today. To get the kind of expanded help you need, however, a multi-volume set will be better. While these sets can be expensive, they will repay your investment with a lifetime of enriched Bible study.

Atlases. A Bible atlas is a volume which sets out maps of the biblical lands and times. While most Bibles have a few maps in their study helps section, an atlas will give you much more detail and discussion. As you are able to locate events geographically, you will better understand their meaning and significance.

For instance, in Jesus' story of the Good Samaritan he tells of a man going "down" from Jerusalem to Jericho. Jesus said this because the road from Jerusalem to Jericho, while only about twenty miles in length, drops in elevation some 3,600 feet. An atlas with elevations will illustrate this clearly.

The more you can picture the geography of biblical events, the more real these events will become to you. A good Bible atlas is therefore an important tool in your study.

Topical Bibles. Another popular tool is a topical Bible—a volume which traces the major topics and themes of the Bible from Genesis to Revelation. If you are preparing a study on the family, for instance, it will help you to have in one place all the biblical references and teachings on the subject. This is what a topical Bible is designed to give you. Some study Bibles, such as the Thompson's Chain-Reference Bible, will give you great topical help. Other volumes, such as Nave's Topical Bible, are devoted only to this approach. For those wanting to understand the larger biblical teachings on specific subjects, a topical Bible is a great help.

Study Bibles. One of the most popular trends in Bible publishing and study today is the "study Bible." A study Bible is any Bible which gives you some kind of study tools along with the text. Most today offer a wide variety of helps, and for this reason have become very popular. Since they give you some of all the tools described above, they are an easy place to begin investing in a Bible study library.

Beware, however, of letting a study Bible be the only source you consult for the more difficult passages. No study Bible can be as thorough in treating a subject or problem as a commentary or other larger volume. When you come across a difficult passage, you will need more options and guidance than a study Bible will have space to give. This is the fault of space limitations, not the author, but it is a problem nonetheless.

Consult a good commentary or two as well. Never give the notes in the study Bible the same authority as the text itself.

An example of this problem is the continued popularity of a particular system of dating which was included in the notes of the first Scofield Bible. This approach teaches that creation began in the year 4004 B.C. As a result in the margin of the first edition of the Scofield Bible beside Genesis 1:1 there appears the date "4004 B.C." This dating method was abandoned in the later editions of the Scofield Bible and is followed by very few today. However, there are still Christians who think that Genesis "teaches" that creation began that year because they read the date in the old Scofield Bible note. Remember that the notes in all study Bibles are the work of fallible men, not the Lord.

Check the opinions found in the study notes against those of other scholars. Most study Bibles are the work of a single individual, and thus express his or her own opinions. No one set of human opinions is the last word on any subject.

A study Bible is a good place to begin building your Bible study library, but only the beginning. The other resources described above will provide guidance no study Bible has space to give. Using each of these tools is an important step in studying the Bible for yourself.

CHECK YOURSELF 4

1. Which is the best practice? (circle your answer)

a. Study the text, then read the commentaries

b. Read one commentary, then study the text, then consult other commentaries and study tools

c. Read several commentaries, then study the text

2. A commentary can hinder your study if you _____
_____.

3. Match the term on the left with the definition on the right:

____ Exegetical   a. Devotes more space to explaining the text

____ Homiletical   b. Devotes more space to the commentary writer's applications

4. Which commentary is best for study purposes? (circle your answer)

a. Exegetical

b. Homiletical

5. T/F: It is best for the commentary writer to give only one option for interpreting a passage, since discussing all the possibilities might confuse the reader.

6. Which tool would you use?

____ You need to find a verse but remember only one or a few of its words.   a. Atlas

____ You need to define a word used in the Bible.   b. Bible Dictionary

____ You need more information on a biblical topic.   c. Concordance

____ You need to know about the geography of a biblical event.   d. Topical Bible

_____ You need to find all the verses in the   e. Bible Encyclopedia
Bible on a specific subject.

A FINAL NOTE

In this chapter we've surveyed the large field of translations and other study helps. These are important tools to help us better understand God's word. However, no work of human knowledge can replace the leadership of the Holy Spirit. You must first depend on Him for guidance. Only then, as He leads, should you turn to the work and wisdom of others.

Martin Luther, one of the most influential preachers and commentators in church history, made this point well. Let's close with his statement, drawn from his personal experience:

> When I was young, I read the Bible over and over again and was so perfectly acquainted with it, that I could, in an instant, have pointed to any verse that might have been mentioned. I then read the commentators, but I soon threw them aside, for I found therein many things my conscience could not approve, as being contrary to the sacred text. 'Tis always better to see with one's own eyes than with those of other people.[15]

The purpose of Bible study is to help you see God in His word, through your own eyes, so that you might know Him personally. Study tools, while valuable, can never substitute for your own work. The more personal your study, the more personal your faith will be.

ANSWERS

CHECK YOURSELF 1

1. c, f, d, a, e, b

CHECK YOURSELF 2

1. manuscripts   2. scholarship   3. archaeology   4. b   5. d

CHECK YOURSELF 3

1. c, a, b   2. d   3. b

CHECK YOURSELF 4

1. a   2. depend on it   3. a, b   4. a   5. F   6. c, b, e, a, d

6

WHAT CAN I LEARN FROM OTHERS?

The Study of God's Word in the Past

B ible study has always been central to Jewish and Christian faith. For this reason, the study of the Scriptures has a long and fascinating history. As we learn how others have approached Bible study in the past, we can find important and practical lessons which will help us study God's word today. Since so much has been written on this subject, we will focus our study only on those past methods which still influence many people today.[1]

THE JEWISH ERA

The New Testament church began with the Hebrew Scriptures, and used Hebrew methods of interpreting them. It is therefore important that we survey Jewish Bible study approaches, so that we can understand their influence in the church then and today.

Ezra—The Beginning of Hermeneutics

The science of biblical interpretation is usually traced in the Bible to Ezra. The Jews had long followed God's commandment to teach the Scriptures to their children and community (see Deut. 11:18–20). But prior to Ezra's time Bible study had not been developed into a discipline of its own.

Ezra lived during a strategic time in Hebrew history. The Jews had returned from exile in Babylon to rebuild their city and nation in Judea. Ezra, a priest and scribe, has become their spiritual leader. After completing the rebuilding of the walls of Jerusalem under Nehemiah's leadership, the people asked Ezra to bring out "the Book of the Law of Moses" to read to them (Neh. 8:1).

Ezra read the Law aloud from daybreak until noon, in the presence of all who could understand. Religious leaders helped Ezra to instruct the people. In summary, "They read from the Book of the Law of God, making it clear and giving the meaning so that the people could understand what was being read" (Neh. 8:8). Since most of the Jewish people had forgotten the Hebrew language during their long exile in Babylon, Ezra and his assistants translated the Hebrew text into Aramaic, their common language.

They read the text aloud to them, and explained its meaning. With this activity, Ezra initiated the work of biblical interpretation.

Bible study in our day still follows Ezra's basic pattern. Like the Hebrews, any of us who cannot read the Bible in its original languages must use a translation. And we all benefit from the help of scholars who explain and apply the meaning of the text. In this sense, Ezra initiated the preaching and Bible study practices followed in Christian churches to this day.

The Qumran Community—Text Without Context

From about 130 B.C. to A.D. 70, a Jewish sect withdrew from the outside world to live in a community known as Qumran, three-fourths of a mile from the northwestern edge of the Dead Sea.

Theirs was a life of strict devotion to God, and their most important activity was copying and studying God's word. The scrolls they left in their caves were discovered in 1947 and are known today as the Dead Sea Scrolls. They are the most ancient Old Testament manuscripts we possess, a thousand years older than anything known prior to their discovery.

The Qumran community wrote multiple commentaries on Scripture, applying the Law to all aspects of their communal lives. However, their interpretations were often made without reference to the original context or meaning of the text. By explaining the Law only with reference to their group, they frequently misinterpreted its intended sense. Theirs was a "text without a context."

In addition, their applications usually strongly emphasized eschatology—the study of the future. The community apparently believed fervently in the coming victory of the Lord on earth and read the Bible in its light. Unfortunately, they often misapplied the text in their desire to emphasize this future hope.

The Qumran community demonstrates today the danger of applying the Bible to our needs today without first learning its original meaning. Remember, "the text can never mean what it never meant."

THE RABBINIC SCHOOLS—RULES FOR BIBLE STUDY

In the years immediately preceding the coming of Christ, Jewish Bible study revolved around two great teachers: Hillel and Shammai. Hillel (60 B.C.–A.D.20?) was an eminent scholar and rabbi ("teacher") in Jerusalem. He gathered a school of disciples to himself, and taught them the Scriptures in accord with set principles of interpretation and a somewhat free method of application. By contrast, Shammai (50 B.C.–A.D. 30) advocated a stricter approach to Bible study which adhered rigidly to the letter of the Law.

Hillel's interpretive principles were especially influential in Jewish and early Christian teaching methods. One of these "rules" is commonly found in the New Testament: the "qal wahomer" (literally, "the light and heavy"). This rule states that whatever applies in a lesser case will always apply in the greater case as well. This became a common rabbinic teaching method and was used often by Jesus.

For instance, consider His parable about the unjust judge whose favor was won by the persistent pleas of a widow (Luke 18:1–7). Taken at first reading, the parable seems to imply that God is unjust, and that He will only help us when we plead with Him in prayer. In fact, this is a "qal wahomer"—if an unjust judge would hear the pleas of a widow, *how much more* will our loving, righteous Father hear our prayers. For other examples of this teaching technique by Jesus, see Matthew 7:9–11 and Luke 11:5–13.

The contrast between Hillel and Shammai is illustrated by a Gentile who came to Shammai and challenged him to teach him the whole Law while the Gentile stood on one foot. Shammai, doubting his sincerity and realizing the impossibility of teaching the letter of the Law in such circumstances, drove the man away with a measuring stick. The Gentile then appeared before Hillel, who said, "What is hateful to you, do not to your neighbour: that is the whole Torah, while the rest is the commentary thereof; go and learn it."[2]

Perhaps the major problem with the rabbinic schools' study methods was their intense devotion to the details of the text. In pressing the rules for Bible study which they developed, the rabbis sometimes dissected the text but lost its overall sense.

For instance, they assigned numeric values to Hebrew consonants, creating interpretations which have no basis in the text. One example is Eliezer, Abraham's servant (Gen. 15:2). The sum of the numbers of his name is 318, the same number as the trained fighting men in Abraham's household. On this basis, it was taught that Eliezer was worth an entire host of soldiers to Abraham, and therefore worthy of inheriting Abraham's household (Gen. 15:3).

The rabbinic schools show us both positive and negative Bible study methods today. On the positive side, we can follow their example in developing and following good procedures for biblical interpretation. We will study this subject in the next chapter. On the negative side, we should beware of pressing the details of Scripture to the point that we miss its overall truths.

RABBINIC LITERATURE—INTERPRETATION BY COMMENTARY

The intense interest in Bible study which the rabbis created in their followers led to massive efforts to interpret and apply the Scriptures. These efforts largely fell into four categories.

First, there was the "midrash," a kind of running commentary on the text. The three oldest are on the Pentateuch: the "Mekilta" on Exodus, "Sifra" on Leviticus, and "Sifre" on Numbers and Deuteronomy. These are comments on the text which treat it in what we would call a "verse-by-verse" format today.

Second, there was the "mishna," a commentary on the text which arranged it by topics. The six major divisions here were (1) agriculture, (2) festivals, (3) women, (4) property rights and legal proceedings, (5) the temple; and (6) laws of purity.

These were treated by compiling all the relevant texts and commenting on them together. We would call this "topical" Bible study today.

Third, there was the "halakah" and the "haggadah." The "halakah" discussed legal matters in Scripture, while the "haggadah" was more a devotional, practical application of the text. The "halakah" would be called an "exegetical" or "critical" commentary, and the "haggadah" a "devotional" commentary today.

Fourth, there was the "gemara," commentaries on the earlier "mishna." The "mishna" and the "gemara" together were compiled into the "Talmud."

Thus the rabbis created commentaries of various types, and then wrote commentaries on their commentaries. The unfortunate result was that the Jewish people often were not taught the Scripture itself. In the rabbis' focus upon their commentaries, they sometimes neglected the very text they were to interpret.

The scribes and teachers often taught the people the words of other scribes and teachers, losing the authority of God's own word. As a result, when Jesus began to teach in their synagogues, "the people were amazed at his teaching, because he taught them as one who had authority, not as the teachers of the law" (Mark 1:22).

Today the rabbinic literature offers us fascinating insights into the ways first-century Jews interpreted their Scriptures. And this literature stands as a constant reminder to us: the purpose of Bible study is Bible study. We are to use commentaries, not to depend on them.

Paul rebuked the Corinthian Christians as spiritual infants who depended on milk when they should have been mature believers, digesting solid food (1 Cor. 3:1–2). Milk is digested food. The mother eats the solid food and digests it so her baby can consume it. In the same way, when a pastor or teacher studies the text and then comments on it for the people, this commentary is "digested" Scripture. While helpful, it is no substitute for the "meat" of the text itself.

Alexandrian Judaism — Seeking the "Spiritual" Meaning

Alexandria, Egypt, was a leading center of Greek culture centuries before the time of Jesus. Here Greek philosophy was taught and promoted widely. A major concept in Greek thought was the separation of the "spiritual" from the "material." Plato (427–327 B.C.) believed that the "ideal" world is spiritual, while our physical world is only its imperfect "shadow" or poor reflection. Therefore, he taught that we should seek the higher "spiritual" truths and not focus on this lower world.

Taking this approach to the Bible, the Jews in Alexandria began seeking ways to discover "spiritual" truths in the "material" text. This method, called "allegory," focuses on hidden or spiritual meanings in the literal words. Philo (ca. 20 B.C.–50 A.D.) was the foremost advocate of this approach. He considered the literal meaning of the text to be helpful only for the immature. The mature disciple would want to find the "higher" spiritual truths of Scripture.

Philo advanced several rules for deciding if a text should be interpreted allegorically. For instance, if the literal says something unworthy of God in the interpreter's opinion, if it seems to contradict something else in Scripture, if it uses unneeded words or repeats something already known, or if there are any abnormalities or symbols present, then it should be treated allegorically. By applying these rules, Philo found many passages for which he used his method.

One famous example of Philo's approach is his interpretation of Abraham's journey to Palestine. According to him, Abraham symbolizes a philosopher. When he comes to Haran (the word means "holes"), he discovers the emptiness of learning by the holes, i.e., the senses. According to Philo, Abraham's journey teaches us the spiritual truth that learning cannot be gained from the physical world.[3]

The allegorical method of Bible study is, unfortunately, still very popular today. Any time a preacher or teacher suggests a "spiritual" meaning which is not intended by the author of the text, he or she is moving toward allegory.

The point of Bible study is to learn what the Bible intends to say. God's word teaches more spiritual, life-transforming truth than we will ever understand or communicate. We need not look for spiritual lessons where they are not intended.

SUMMARY

Jewish Bible study began with Ezra, focusing on the literal interpretation of God's word. Soon, however, some began to apply the text to their lives without considering its intended meaning.

Along the way, rules were developed to aid in the study of Scripture. Unfortunately, these rules sometimes became more the focus of study than the text they were supposed to interpret. As Greek philosophy influenced Hebrew thinking, many Jews began to depart from the literal meaning in search of higher "spiritual" truths. Each of these approaches to Bible study is still followed by some today. Popularity, however, is no guarantee that a method is right.

CHECK YOURSELF I

1. Match the following:

____	Ezra	a.	Seeking the "spiritual" meaning of the text
____	Qumran	b.	Rules for Bible study
____	Rabbinic schools	c.	The beginning of biblical interpretation
____	Rabbinic literature	d.	Interpreting the text without reference to its original context or meaning
____	Alexandrian Judaism	e.	Intepretation by commentary

THE PATRISTIC AGE

"Patra" is Latin for "father." The "Patristic" period is the period of the fathers of the church, approximately A.D. 100–500. Many of the most significant trends in biblical interpretation today can be traced to this era.

FINDING CHRIST IN THE OLD TESTAMENT

The first problem in Bible study for the early pastors and teachers was how to use the Old Testament in the church. Their typical approach was to find Christ in the Hebrew Scriptures wherever possible. To do this, they often resorted to the allegorical method, seeking spiritual truths beyond the literal meaning of the text. Let's look at some examples.

First, consider *Clement of Rome* (A.D. 30–100). This was probably the Clement Paul names as one of his companions at Philippi (Phil. 4:3), and was one of the early leaders of the church at Rome. In his desire to find Christ in the Old Testament, he made much use of allegory. Commenting on Rahab's scarlet rope which she hung from her window (Josh. 2:21), Clement says,

> And thus they made it manifest that redemption should flow through the blood of the Lord to all them that believe and hope in God. Ye see, beloved, that there was not only faith, but prophecy, in this woman.[4]

The *Epistle of Barnabas* is another example. Not written by the New Testament Barnabas, it commonly uses allegory to find Christian truths in the Old Testament. For instance, commenting on the dietary laws of the Jews, the author says,

> "Thou shalt not eat the hyena." He means, "Thou shalt not be an adulterer, nor a corrupter, nor be like to them that are such." Wherefore? Because that animal annually changes its sex, and is at one time male, and at another female.[5]

Justin Martyr (ca. 100–167) was one of the early church's greatest heroes and leaders. His defense of Christian truth against the attacks of pagan philosophers won him wide appreciation among his brethren. Unfortunately, he sometimes resorted to erroneous interpretations to find Christ in the Old Testament. For instance, he insisted that the high priest's bells on his robe (Ex. 28:33–35) symbolize the twelve apostles who "ring out" the gospel of the Great High Priest.[6]

A different approach to the Christian use of the Old Testament was that of *Marcion* (born ca. 100). As we saw in our discussion of the canon, Marcion was rejected by the church as a heretic. He rejected the Old Testament, and accepted only Luke and Paul's letters in the New. His method of treating the Hebrew Scriptures was basically to ignore them.

Irenaeus (born ca. 130) offered what later became the official approach of the church to the Old Testament, namely, that the church itself is the only correct medium of biblical interpretation. He insisted that both the Old and New Testaments are rightly understood only through the teachings of official church leaders.

And so in the earliest period of Christian Bible study, we encounter the spiritualizing approach of allegory, the rejection of what conflicts with our theology, and the doctrine that only the church can interpret the text. Unfortunately, all three methods are still popular in Bible study today.

THE TRIUMPH OF ALLEGORY

With *Clement of Alexandria* (150–213?), the allegorical approach to the Bible became a fully-developed system of interpretation. Clement believed that there are five senses to Scripture: the historical (the actual event), the doctrinal (its obvious teachings), the prophetic (its predictions), the philosophical (underlying meanings of the text), and the mystical (its deepest moral or spiritual truths, symbolized by the historical). He taught his students how to discover all five senses in any text.

One well-known example of Clement's approach is his interpretation of Psalm 150. Here the different musical instruments are taken to symbolize the human body, such as the lyre for the "mouth struck by the Spirit." Commenting on "Praise him with the timbrel and the dance," Clement says that this "refers to the Church meditating on the resurrection of the dead in the resounding skin."[7] Clement's most famous pupil was *Origen* (185–251?). Origen was a scholar of the first rank, a prolific author, and an interpreter committed to the allegorical approach.

Interpreting Jesus' parable of the laborers in the vineyard (Matt. 20:1-16), Origen taught that the laborers' day stands for the history of the world, and its hours mark the principal divisions of mankind's spiritual history.[8]

Origen furthered the allegorical approach with the "threefold method," a model which endured for centuries. Taken from 1 Thessalonians 5:23—"May your whole spirit, soul and body be kept blameless at the coming of our Lord Jesus Christ"—he taught that all Scripture has the same three senses. The "body" is the external event described in Scripture, the literal sense. The "soul" describes our personal relationships, the moral sense.

The "spirit" indicates our relationship with God, the mystical sense. This, he said, is the most important sense in Scripture. In intepreting Jesus' triumphant entry into Jerusalem, Origen taught that Jesus' colt is the Old Testament which carries him to the cross, and the two apostles who contained the animal and brought it to Christ are the moral and spiritual senses.[9]

EFFORTS TO RESTORE A LITERAL APPROACH

Not all scholars in this period succumbed to the spiritualizing approach of allegory. In fact, a notable attempt to return interpretation to the literal sense was made by the School of Antioch. Under Theophilus of Antioch (115–188), Diodorus of Tarsus (d. 393), Theodor of Mopsuestia (350–428) and Chrysostom (354–407), this school of scholars approached the Bible in a much more literal way than their contemporaries.

Theodor of Mopsuestia argued that an Old Testament prophecy should only be interpreted messianically if it is used in this way in the New Testament. Unfortunately, the more literal approach of Theodor and his colleagues never gained enough influence to prevent the wide use of allegory in the medieval church.[10]

Another example of one who emphasized the literal sense is *Jerome* (347–420). He is most famous in church history for the "Vulgate," his translation of the Bible into Latin. However, he was also a leading advocate of the literal approach to Scripture.

So, while the allegorical method became pervasive in the early centuries of the church, the literal approach was never completely lost. It remained for Augustine to combine the two into principles of interpretation which were followed for a thousand years.

AUGUSTINE — PRINCIPLES OF INTERPRETATION

Augustine of Hippo (354–430) was the leading intellectual of the Patristic Age and one of the greatest Christian scholars of all time. Augustine combined the allegorical approach of Greek philosophy with the more literal methods current in his day, developing twelve principles for Bible study. Among these, the most important for us are:

1. The necessity of Christian faith for interpretation

2. The priority of the literal and historical senses of the text

3. The importance of the original intent of the biblical author

4. An emphasis on the context of the text

5. The importance of using clear passages to interpret the more difficult

6. The necessity of education for interpretation.

Unfortunately, Augustine also accepted allegory when the text could possess more than one meaning. In addition, he found undue significance in biblical numbers and argued for the need to consult the church creeds in interpretation.

In his biblical studies, Augustine could be as allegorical as Origen. For instance, in treating the parable of the Good Samaritan he interpreted the oil and wine to be baptism, and the inn to be the Church.[11] He took Psalm 104:19, "the sun knows when to go down," to refer to Jesus' death and burial.[12]

Nevertheless, the principles for Bible study Augustine developed are still valid and useful today. To sum up, in the first five centuries of the church, various Bible study methods were suggested which are still in popular use. Allegorical interpretation sought spiritual truths which were beyond the literal intent of the author; more literal methods were developed and advocated; and comprehensive principles for the study of Scripture were created. Most Bible study for the next thousand years of the church stood on these foundations.

CHECK YOURSELF 2

1. The most popular way to find Christ in the Old Testament was through the use of the _____ method.

2. In Origen's method, match:

   ____ body   a. mystical sense

_____ soul   b. literal sense

_____ spirit   c. moral sense

3. The School of Antioch emphasized a return to the _____ sense of Scripture.

The Middle Ages

The period of church history which begins with the death of Augustine and culminates in the Reformation is usually called the "medieval" period or the "middle ages." While the trends just discussed were greatly developed during this period, not many new approaches were attempted. As regards biblical interpretation, this period was largely a time of transition. Let's look briefly at those developments which have endured in significance.[13]

Approaches to Bible Study

Four methods from the Middle Ages are still influential today. First was the "catena," a series or chain of interpretations put together on the basis of earlier commentaries by church fathers. This approach to Bible study is akin to the old Jewish approach of commenting on the commentaries, as in the Talmud. It remains a popular method of Bible study and preaching.

Second was the "gloss," a word of interpretation or comment inserted within and beside the biblical text. This kind of running commentary is a precursor to the verse-by-verse study Bibles popular today.

Third was the development of schools of Scripture study, each promoting its own approach to the Bible. These schools are precursors to the development of modern academic and vocational seminaries.

Fourth was the further development of allegorical methods. By this time every verse of Scripture was held to possess four meanings. To illustrate these, consider Galatians 4:21–31 and Paul's symbolic use of "Jerusalem." The city was interpreted in four ways: historically, as the city of the Jews; allegorically (symbolically), as the church of Christ; anagogically (in terms of the future), as the heavenly city; and tropologically (morally), as the human soul. As we have already seen, this misguided search for the deeper "spiritual" meaning in every text is still popular.

THOMAS OF AQUINAS—THE PRIORITY OF THE LITERAL

Without doubt the leading figure of the medieval church was *Thomas of Aquinas* (1224?–74). Thomas did more to develop the systematic theology of Roman Catholicism than any other person, and his thought and methods are still influential. Regarding his approach to Bible study, one major principle stands above all others: the priority of the literal sense of Scripture. As Thomas says,

> Our faith rests upon the revelation made to the apostles and prophets, who wrote the canonical books, and not on the revelations (if any such there are) made to other doctors.[14]

As the literal, intended sense of the Bible is its first meaning, other senses can only be interpreted on this basis. According to Thomas, the reader must not find other meanings which violate the stated, literal text. Again, in Thomas' words,

> That first meaning whereby words signify things belongs to the first sense, the historical or literal. That meaning whereby things signified by words have themselves also a meaning is called the spiritual sense, which is based on the literal, and presupposes it.[15]

Thomas does allow for allegory in interpreting the Old Testament, the "tropological" in finding moral precepts in the New Testament, and the "anagogical" in studying eternal, future topics. However, he calls for these to be grounded in the literal, intended meaning of the biblical author. In this way, he laid the foundation for interpretation methods which were to follow.

NICHOLAS OF LYRA—A BRIDGE TO THE REFORMATION

One other figure deserves mention in even a brief sketch of medieval Bible study—*Nicholas of Lyra* (1270–1340). Nicholas drew heavily upon Jewish scholarship and tended to interpret Scripture in terms of its historical, intended meaning. While he accepted the "multiple sense" approach, he argued that the other senses must be built upon the literal.

Nicholas is especially important to the history of Bible study for influencing Martin Luther and the reformers to come. Luther studied at the University of Erfurt, where Nicholas's system of interpretation prevailed, and it has been said that "if Lyra had not played, Luther would not have danced." Luther's commentary on Genesis also demonstrates dependence on Nicholas's methods. With Nicholas we can see further preparation for an emphasis on the literal sense of Scripture, one of the primary features of the Reformation.

Check Yourself 3

1. Match the term on the left with the definition on the right:

____	Catena	a.	Finding moral precepts in the New Testament
____	Gloss	b.	Studying eternal, future topics
____	Tropological	c.	A word of interpretation or comment inserted within and beside the biblical text
____	Anagogical	d.	A chain of intepretations put together on the basis of earlier commentaries by church fathers

2. Nicholas of Lyra is especially important in the history of Bible study for his influence of _____ and the reformers to come.

The Reformation

At the dawn of the sixteenth century, biblical interpretation was still largely governed by the four-fold sense of Scripture.

By the end of this century, the landscape of hermeneutics had changed dramatically and forever. Many replaced the allegorical method with a literal approach to Scripture. A movement to grant the individual freedom to study the Bible stood opposed to the centuries-old practice of interpreting by church councils and creeds.

For many believers, the Bible alone was seen as our authority under God. All this was the result of the movement we call the "Reformation."

MARTIN LUTHER — PRINCIPLES FOR BIBLE STUDY

The beginning of the actual Reformation movement is usually traced to *Martin Luther* (1483–1546). Luther's theology became foundational for the Reformation. Luther developed six principles for Bible study which are still followed by most Protestants today:

1. The "psychological" principle: the need for spiritual commitment. Luther argued that God reveals the true meaning of His word by the Spirit to His people (see 1 Cor. 2:11–12).

2. The "authority" principle: the Bible stands above church authority and judges the creeds and opinions of men.

3. The "literal" principle: Bible study must emphasize the historical and grammatical meaning of the text, and reject all allegory and the "four-fold" method.

4. The "sufficiency" principle: the Bible is a clear book and can be interpreted by all Christians. Here Luther stood for the "priesthood of every believer" in opposition to interpretation by clergy alone.

5. The "Christological" principle: the purpose of all Bible study is to find and trust in Christ.

6. The "law-gospel" principle: the Old Testament law was given to judge sin, and then New Testament grace was given to atone for it. We must never de-emphasize the unlawfulness of sin, or make grace into law and human works.

These six principles were and are crucial to Protestant biblical interpretation.

JOHN CALVIN — THE SCIENTIFIC STUDY OF SCRIPTURE

The first so-called scientific interpreter of the Bible was the reformer *John Calvin* (1509–64). Calvin's background was in legal studies, and he brought this systematic approach to the Scriptures.

He especially insisted that "Scripture interprets Scripture," arguing that we should study the grammar, history, and context of the passage rather than reading into it our own opinions. Calvin greatly developed and advanced the Protestant method of grammatical and historical interpretation.

The Council of Trent—Roman Catholic Creedalism

In response to the Protestant movements described above, the Roman Catholic church met for eighteen years in the official Council of Trent (1545–63). The result was a narrowly defined creed of orthodoxy which claimed that church teachings and creeds are the basis for all correct Bible study. The stage was now set for two basic schools of thought: interpretation by any believer, based on the literal text; and interpretation by priest and church official, based on church teachings. These two approaches have dominated Christian theology for the last four centuries.

The Anabaptists and Other Reformers

Another strain in the sixteenth-century Reformation was the "Anabaptists." The movement began in Switzerland, and still influences some Protestant churches and theology today. The name is taken from the Greek word "ana," meaning "re"; an "Anabaptist" is thus a "re-baptizer." This points to an important doctrine, held by Baptists and many other Protestant denominations, that one should be baptized by immersion and only upon personal commitment to Christ.

The Anabaptists' doctrine of baptism is not, however, their only contribution to Protestant theology. Their view of the Bible and its study, held in common with many other reforming groups, has also been helpful for millions of Christians across recent centuries. This method of Bible study can be condensed into five principles:

1. "Sola scriptura"—the Bible is our sole authority in faith and practice.

2. A de-emphasis of creeds—we should emphasize the text itself.

3. A "Christological" approach—Christ fulfills and interprets the Bible.

4. The New Testament as our rule for faith and practice—the Old Testament should be interpreted in light of the New.

5. The right of the individual in interpretation—the believer is free to study the Bible apart from church authority.

In summary, we can list several Reformation Bible study principles which are still followed by most Protestants today:

- the need for spiritual commitment by the reader

- the literal method of Bible study (the "grammatical-historical" approach)

- the authority of the Bible above church doctrines or creeds

- the right of the individual to interpret the Scripture

- the Christological purpose and focus for Bible study

- the affirmation of the New Testament as our rule for faith and practice.

As we will see in the next chapter, these Reformation tenets still form the foundation for our Bible study today.

CHECK YOURSELF 4

1. Match the following Reformation principles and definitions:

____ Sola scriptura   a. The Bible is fulfilled and best understood in Christ.

____ Christological interpretive approach   b. Bible study must emphasize the historical and grammatical meaning of the text.

____ Priesthood of the believer   c. The Bible is our sole authority in faith and practice.

____ Literal method of Bible study   d. The Bible stands above and judges church creeds and the opinions of men.

_____ Authority principle   e. Each Christian has the right to
                                 interpret the Bible without church
                                 creed or authority.

The Modern Era

The last four hundred years have seen remarkable interest in the subject of the Bible and hermeneutics. For our purposes, we will highlight only those movements which might influence your Bible study today.[16]

Modern Liberalism — Subjective Interpretation

One of these key movements is often called "liberalism." In the dictionary sense of the word, this is an intellectual method which is free from any tradition or external authority. In Bible study, liberalism basically grants one the freedom to interpret the text as he or she wishes. This is the "subjective" approach. By contrast, the "objective" method insists that the text possesses an objective, intended meaning, whether the reader interprets it correctly or not.

Two names are essential to our study: Immanuel Kant (1724–1804) and Friedrich Schleiermacher (1768–1834). Kant remains one of the most important thinkers in Western history. The problem he addressed is basic to life: what is the relationship of our minds to our sense impressions? Some said that all truth comes from intellectual processes; others said it comes from sense experiences. Kant wed the two approaches, teaching that the mind interprets sense data and this results in knowledge.

This seemingly simple idea led to a crucial conclusion: you and I cannot know anything as it is, only our experience of it. According to Kant, you cannot know this book, only how it looks to you. I might see its color or feel its pages differently than you would. As a result, all we can know about reality is our experience of it, not the "thing in itself."

Schleiermacher applied this idea to theology and the Bible, with this devastating result: you and I cannot know God, only our experience of Him. In this approach, the Bible becomes only a record of the religious experiences of others, not a book of objective truth. And the way you will interpret the Bible through your experience will differ from my interpretation. As a result, for those in this method there cannot be objective Bible study or theology. They consider biblical truth, like all knowledge, to be subjective. For this approach, Schleiermacher is considered today the "father of modern liberalism."

The subjective approach to Scripture, reading the Bible through our own experiences, has produced many unfortunate results for its followers. One is that if we have not experienced the supernatural, then we are free to dismiss the supernatural from Scripture. Many interpreters have thus denied the miraculous, reinterpreting it as symbols or myths. One such scholar refers repeatedly to the resurrection, Jesus' appearance on the road to Emmaus, and the stories of the empty tomb as "legends."[17]

Another result is that the Bible is valued only for its ethical content. If we have no objective truth to preach, we are left only with ethical principles to suggest. Jesus thus becomes a teacher of morals, and Christianity only an ethical system. Of course, Jesus claims objective truth for himself (John 14:6). The Bible promises that we can know God with certainty (1 John 5:13). God's word offers us the objective experience of salvation on the basis of his objective word:

> For you have been born again, not of perishable seed, but of imperishable, through the living and enduring word of God. For, "All men are like grass, and all their glory is like the flowers of the field; the grass withers and the flowers fall, but the word of the Lord stands forever." And this is the word that was preached to you (1 Pet. 1:23–25).

As someone has suggested, my denying the sunrise doesn't disprove the sun, it only proves my ignorance. Likewise, denying the objective truth of Scripture doesn't disprove the Bible, it only proves my misunderstanding of God and His word.

A warning: those who accept the objective authority of the Bible still must guard against the same results in study as those of modern liberalism. If you believe the Bible is objectively true, but interpret it apart from its intended meaning, you arrive at your own subjective conclusions. Thus you can unfortunately be conservative in your view of Scripture and "liberal" in interpreting it.

PRINCETON THEOLOGY—RATIONAL, TOPICAL BIBLE STUDY

Charles Hodge (1797–1878) led a conservative response to the modern liberal movement. His movement centered in Princeton Seminary and is thus known as "Princeton theology."

This approach defends the Bible as rational truth. It takes Scripture to be a book of objective facts about the Christian faith and life. It then seeks to arrange these facts into a systematic unity. From this approach, one can arrange the various verses of the Bible into a unified "doctrine of God," "doctrine of man," "doctrine of the church," etc.

This approach of arranging the Scriptures into systems of doctrine remains a very influential method of Bible study and preaching today. In a more popular application, you have perhaps heard a preacher take a topic and arrange verses from many different texts on this subject into a sermon. This is often called "topical" preaching, as opposed to "expository" preaching which develops primarily a single text.

One difficulty with the topical approach is that its practitioners sometimes take the different verses out of their context and originally intended meaning, arranging them to teach something none of the individual verses was intended to say.

This clearly was not the intent or practice of Hodge and his theological school, but it is sometimes the result of misusing their methods. Misarranging verses into a meaning none of their authors intended is called "false combinationalism." For example, one could take Psalm 23:5, "You prepare a table before me in the presence of my enemies," and combine it with verse 6, "I will dwell in the house of the Lord forever." The result might be, "my enemies are in the house of the Lord." While this may sometimes be true, it is obviously not what David intended to say.

It is clear that the Bible is true, and that it teaches truth. But we must always be careful to interpret this truth consistent with its intended meaning, or we use truth to teach falsehood.

DISPENSATIONALISM—INTERPRETING BY BIBLICAL PERIODS

John Darby (1800–82) and his followers developed a new method of Bible study which is still tremendously popular today: "dispensationalism." A dispensation is defined as a period of time in history and the Bible. This method teaches that the different parts of the Bible must be interpreted according to their place in the overall system of dispensations. One typical organization is the dispensations of:

- innocence—Genesis 1:28–3:6

- conscience—Genesis 4:1–8:14

- civil government—Genesis 8:15–11:9

- promise [to Abraham]—Genesis 11:10–Exodus 18:27

- Mosaic law—Exodus 18:28–Acts 1:26

- grace [the present dispensation]—Acts 2:1–Revelation 19:21

- the millennium—Revelation 20.

This method stands on two crucial principles: the separation of Israel and the church, and a thorough-going literal approach. Dispensationalists believe that every promise to Israel not yet fulfilled will one day be fulfilled literally. Non-dispensationalists often see these promises as fulfilled in the church. And dispensationalists approach the Bible very literally, including Revelation and other parts which nondispensationalists may see as more symbolic in nature.

Dispensationalism has been promoted especially by the Scofield Bible and the Ryrie Study Bible. It is taught at several Bible institutes in this country and is popular with many pastors and laypeople today.

THE INSTITUTIONAL MODEL—INTERPRETING BY CREEDS

Another movement which still influences Bible study today can be called "institutionalism." This is Bible study by the creeds of a certain religious institution or movement. While traceable to Irenaeus and still popular with many Roman Catholics today, this approach is not confined to Catholicism. If Bible study is made subservient to man-made definitions or creeds, Scripture then serves our theological opinions.

As we saw earlier, the "priesthood of the believer" guarantees every interpreter the right to approach the Bible for himself or herself. So long as we seek the author's intended meaning and use proper methods, we do not need human institutions or dogmas to interpret the Bible for us. While the opinions of others will often be very helpful in our own Bible study, they should never substitute for it.

This principle has relevance for nearly every student of Scripture. For those in more creedally-oriented denominations, it means that their denominational statements and doctrines will not prevent their studying the Bible themselves. For those in less creedal denominations, it means that they will not depend on their pastor, Sunday School teacher, or commentaries to study the Scripture for them. For all of us, it means that we will seek to encounter God personally and daily in His word.

CHECK YOURSELF 5

1. Match the person on the left with the description on the right:

____ Immanuel Kant   a. Princeton theology, defending the
                           Bible as rational truth.

____ Friedrich   b. All we can know about reality is our
     Schleiermacher   experience of it.

____ Charles Hodge   c. Dispensationalism

____ John Darby   d. All we can know of God is our
                           experience of him—the Bible is a
                           record of the religious experiences
                           of others

2. For the subjective approach, circle the statement which does not apply:

   a. One is free to interpret the text according to personal experience.

   b. The miraculous can be reinterpreted as myth or legend.

   c. The text possesses no relevance for Christian faith today.

   d. The Bible is to be valued for its ethical content.

In Summary

The material we have surveyed briefly in this chapter is the subject of multi-volume scholarly studies. Our purpose has been only to highlight those trends in the history of Bible study which most affect popular study of Scripture today. We may place the methods into one of the two catagories.

Approaches to Avoid

- Applying the Bible to our needs without first learning its intended meaning (Qumran)

- Interpreting by commentary (Rabbinic literature)

- Seeking an underlying "spiritual" meaning beyond the literal sense of the text (allegory)

- Making the church and its officials the only proper interpreters of Scripture (Irenaeus, institutionalism, creedalism)

- Subjective interpretation (modern "liberalism")

Approaches to Follow:

- Sound procedures for Bible study (Rabbinic schools)

- Basing interpretation on the literal sense of Scripture (Thomas, Luther and Reformation theology)

- The need for spiritual commitment (Luther, the Anabaptists)

- Holding the Bible above church authority (the Reformers)

- The belief that all Christians can interpret God's word for themselves (the Reformers)

- Centering all interpretation in Christ, leading to faith in Him (Anabaptists)

In our last chapter, we will build on this historical foundation by constructing a method of Bible study which will help you study any text in God's word.

ANSWERS

CHECK YOURSELF 1

1. c, d, b, e, a

CHECK YOURSELF 2

1. allegorical   2. b, c, a   3. literal

CHECK YOURSELF 3

1. d, c, a, b   2. Martin Luther

CHECK YOURSELF 4

1. c, a, e, b, d

CHECK YOURSELF 5

1. b, d, a, c,   2. c

7

HOW CAN I LEARN
FOR MYSELF?

Studying God's Word Today

O n the grounds of Hampton Court in London is a maze of
bushes planted to form solid walls, head high. In the center,
on a high platform, sits a guide. When people get lost
working their way through the maze, they look up to the guide, who
points them to their next move.

God's word is our guide for Christian living. But as with any guide,
we must follow its directions correctly. If our guide points north and
we turn south, we will be lost, no matter how accurate our guide's
directions.

Now we come to the most practical part of this book: methods of
personal Bible study. We will look at those principles which will guide
us in interpreting any text in the word of God. When we have finished
this discussion, you will have learned to use principles which will help
you get more from any part of God's word.[1]

Personal Preparations

You must with three personal, spiritual commitments before any approach to Bible study can be effective.

You Need a Personal Relationship with God

First, you must know the Lord personally, through the Holy Spirit. The apostle Paul made this requirement clear:

> The Spirit searches all things, even the deep things of God. For who among men knows the thoughts of a man except the man's spirit within him? In the same way no one knows the thoughts of God except the Spirit of God. . . . The man without the Spirit does not accept the things that come from the Spirit of God, for they are foolishness to him, and he cannot understand them, because they are spiritually discerned. (1 Cor. 2:10–11,14)

This text does not say that an uncoverted reader can understand nothing of the Bible. But it does mean that the reader will not accept and apply the truths of Scripture apart from the leading of the Spirit. Their intended application will be ignored or rejected unless the Holy Spirit does His work of conviction and guidance. John Piper states this fact well:

> It takes the Holy Spirit to make us docile to the Bible. The work of the Holy Spirit in the process of interpretation is not to add information, but to give to us the discipline to study and the humility to accept the truth we find without twisting it.[2]

In order to understand and apply the word of God, you must first know God. Augustine called the Bible the Father's "letters from home." We must read the Scriptures out of a personal relationship with their Author.

You Must Work Hard

Second, you must be willing to work and study hard. Paul's word to Timothy applies to every Bible student: "Devote yourself to the public reading of Scripture, to preaching and to teaching" (1 Tim. 4:13). "Devote yourself" translates a Greek word which implies previous, private preparations.[3] Reading, preaching, and teaching

God's word all require diligent, personal effort. The available study tools will be a great advantage to you.

Several good Bible translations, a Bible dictionary, a concordance, an atlas, topical Bibles and encyclopedias, and good commentaries are all tremendous helps. Never assume you can do without the support of others, as if to say, "I don't need the help of more than two thousand years of scholarship and interpretation." But use these tools only to assist your study, never to replace it. Never ask another person to do your personal work in God's word. Bible study is serious business and rewards serious discipline.

You Must Obey What You Discover

Last, you must be obedient to the truths you encounter. Jesus said, "If any one chooses to do God's will, he will find out whether my teaching comes from God or whether I speak on my own" (John 7:17). Only when you obey the principles of God's word, applying them personally, do they come to life for you.

As we have seen, the Bible exists to bring us to personal relationship with God in Christ. You must study its words with their life-changing purpose always in mind. Before you open God's word, you must first open your heart to its truth.

Before You Begin

We do not live in a vacuum. Our circumstances and experiences inevitably create in us assumptions which affect the way we view reality. These assumptions or presuppositions are present in all areas of study, including Bible study. It is impossible to approach God's word without them. Instead, we should seek the best presuppositions, the most helpful assumptions, and use them in studying the Scriptures. Three such presuppositions are especially important for the study of God's word.

Scripture Can Be Understood

Our first presupposition is taken from Luther and the Reformers: the Bible can be understood. God's has given His word to us in such a way that any believer can read its pages and discover divine truth.

We do not depend on church, creed, or council to interpret the Scriptures. Because of the "priesthood of the believer," every Christian has the right and responsibility to study the Bible personally.

This means that the methods we will discuss here do not begin with the positions of the church or its creeds. Our approach to Bible study begins with the Bible, not human opinions about it. A balance must be kept: we will seek to learn from the study of others, but we will not begin there. We will start with the text itself, in the belief that it can be understood.

The New Testament Interprets the Old

Our second guiding presupposition is that the New Testament interprets the Old Testament. As we saw in chapter four, the Bible centers in Jesus Christ, and He fulfills the Old Testament (Matt. 5:17). The New Testament, which reveals Christ, is our means of interpreting the Old Testament, which prepares His way.

The New Testament is our norm for studying the Old. Another way to state this principle is by the phrase "progressive revelation." This theological term means that God reveals Himself in Scripture in a way which builds later revelation upon earlier. Upon the foundation of the Law, God speaks through His prophets. They in turn focus on Messiah, who is Himself God's personal revelation. The New Testament builds on this revelation in person by revelation in word. The New Testament is God's fullest revelation of Himself in Christ, and is therefore our means of understanding His earlier revelation.

This presupposition leads to an important principle regarding our interpretation of the Old Testament. Whenever an Old Testament law is renewed in the New Testament, it retains the force of law for Christians today. For instance, by renewing the Ten Commandments, Jesus makes them obligatory for His followers (see Matt. 19:16–19).

On the other hand, any Old Testament law not renewed in the New Testament retains the force of principle for Christian living. For instance, the Jewish dietary codes were made non-binding on Gentile converts by the Jerusalem Council (Acts 15:28–29). However, these laws still demonstrate the relevant principle that God cares about our diet, our bodies, and our health. As you can see, the presupposition that the New Testament interprets the Old is important for our study of much of God's word.

SCRIPTURE INTERPRETS SCRIPTURE

The third foundational presupposition for our Bible study is that the Bible best interprets itself. Because God's word is unified, coherent, and fully inspired, the best way to understand any single passage is to interpret that text in light of the entire Scripture. We will seek throughout our Bible study to compare Scripture with Scripture, interpreting the part by the whole.

Five important principles rest on this guiding presupposition. First, unclear passages should be interpreted in light of clear texts. We should study the difficult parts of Scripture in light of its clear teachings.

For instance, Luke 14:26 contains this difficult statement of Jesus: "If anyone comes to me and does not hate his father and mother, his wife and children, his brothers and sisters—yes, even his own life—he cannot be my disciple." Does this verse mean that Jesus is anti-family? Must we reject those we love the most in order to love Christ? This hard passage is clarified by studying Matthew's version of the same statement of Jesus: "Anyone who loves his father or mother more than me is not worthy of me; anyone who loves his son or daughter more than me is not worthy of me" (Matt. 10:37).

Obviously Luke's version means that we are to "hate" our families only in the sense that we place them under Christ in priority and commitment. The clear version helps us understand the more difficult.

In addition, the New Testament contains other straightforward statements on the importance of family. Peter and other apostles and missionaries bring their wives with them in their ministries (1 Cor. 9:5). Paul warns that one who does not provide for his family "has denied the faith and is worse than an unbeliever" (1 Tim. 5:8). And Paul commands the husband to love his wife as Christ loved the church (Eph. 5:25). These clear references help us understand Jesus' words and apply them today.

Second, no major doctrine should be based only on one verse or a few miscellaneous verses. For example, the "millenium" is found explicitly only in Revelation 20:1–6. While this is obviously an important subject, it should not be made a test of orthodoxy. At least seven theories are held by different Bible-believing scholars on this controversial topic. No person's belief in Scripture should be questioned because of his or her theory on the millenium. We should seek to build major doctrines on the more extensive biblical texts.

Third, passages which are brief should be studied in light of passages of greater length. In other words, we should study a single verse in light of the larger passage in which it is found, this passage in light of its book, and the book in light of the entire Scripture. As we consider the larger counsel of God's word, we allow Scripture to interpret itself.

Fourth, when a doctrine is taught in various parts of Scripture, it applies to all times and cultures. There are many different contexts and circumstances behind the various texts of the Bible. Whenever a statement is found in a variety of different contexts and is taught by a number of biblical authors, we may be sure it is intended as a timeless principle of truth.

Fifth, if two biblical statements appear humanly to contradict, we must accept both. Divine truth is not bound to human logic, and often must be expressed by stating two truths which seem at odds with each other. This is called an "antinomy"—the acceptance of two principles which seem mutually exclusive but are each independently true.

For example, believers are often troubled by the "freedom-divine sovereignty" question. If I have complete freedom of will, does this limit God's knowledge and control of the future? Or, if God knows the future, how can I have freedom of choice?

The fact is, the Bible often states both principles as true: I have free will, and yet God controls all that occurs. For instance, Jesus says, "Are not two sparrows sold for a penny? Yet not one of them will fall to the ground apart from the will of your Father" (Matt. 10:29). But two verses later He calls us to decide: "So don't be afraid; you are worth more than many sparrows" (v. 31). On another occasion Jesus states both principles in one verse: "The Son of Man will go as it has been decreed, but woe to that man who betrays him" (Luke 22:22). When instances such as this occur, we must accept both principles as true.

Because Scripture interprets Scripture, all biblical principles are true, even when they transcend our human logic. God's word can be understood; the New Testament interprets the Old Testament; and

Scripture interprets Scripture. These three presuppositions are vital to all Bible study.

CHECK YOURSELF I

CIRCLE THE BEST CHOICE

1. Because the Bible can be understood, we *do / do not* depend on church creeds to study God's word.

2. The *New / Old* Testament interprets the *New / Old* Testament.

3. Progressive revelation teaches that God reveals himself in Scripture in a way which builds *earlier / later* revelation upon *earlier / later*.

4. *Clear / Unclear* passages should be studied in the light of *clear / unclear* passages.

5. *Brief / Longer* passages should be studied in the light of *brief / longer* passages.

6. Whenever a statement is found in various parts of Scripture, it applies *only to the context / for all time*.

7. If two biblical statements appear humanly to contradict, we must accept *neither / one or the other / both*.

BACKGROUND QUESTIONS

Martin Luther once compared his method of Bible study to gathering apples from an apple tree. First, he said, he would lay hold of the trunk, shake it and collect the fruit that falls to the ground. Then he would climb into the tree and shake each of the larger branches separately. Then he would gather from each separate limb. Then he would inspect each twig. And finally he would look under each leaf to see what else might be found.[4]

In other words, before we can study any particular verse in the Bible, we should first examine the book in which it is found. Only when we are familiar with the trunk can we climb it and harvest its fruit.

It is helpful to first read the entire book in which your text is found, if possible. Note briefly your first impressions and questions about the book, major ideas, and other items of interest. Then you can study the following background questions.

WHO WAS THE WRITER?

First, who was the writer of this text and book? What can you learn about his background and experiences? What are the circumstances in his life at the time of his writing? Knowing the author is critical to understanding his book.

Recently our family inherited some antique furniture. Inside one bureau was a set of very old letters. They were fascinating but also frustrating, for we knew nothing of their author and so could tell little about them. As with any literature, knowing the author is the necessary starting point to understanding his or her words.

WHO ARE THE RECIPIENTS?

The second question follows the first: to whom is the author writing? Are they believers or unbelievers? Persecuted or not? A church, a group of churches, or an individual? What can you learn about their historical and cultural circumstances?

Often you can tell a great deal about both the writer and his recipients from the text itself. For instance, Paul's introduction to his letter to the Philippians names the author (1:1), indicates that he knows his readers personally (1:3), and shows that they are his very special friends (1:5–8). In fact, every one of Paul's letters names both its author and his readers.

Once you have examined the text, next check a good commentary and/or encyclopedia on this question. The information here will be invaluable in your interpretation of the text later.

WHAT IS THE AUTHOR'S PURPOSE?

Now you are ready to examine a vital question: what is the reason for the book? Writing in the ancient world was too hard to do without some compelling purpose. You should know all you can about that purpose, so you can interpret the text properly.

Much of the Bible is "task theology." In other words, it was written to accomplish a specific task or purpose. If you do not know all you can about that purpose at the outset, you'll miss much of what the text intends to say.

Often the text will make its purpose clear. For instance, Luke defines his reason for writing at the outset:

> Many have undertaken to draw up an account of the things that have been fulfilled among us, just as they were handed down to us by those who from the first were eyewitnesses and servants of the word. Therefore, since I myself have carefully investigated everything from the beginning, it seemed good also to me to write an orderly account for you, most excellent Theophilus, so that you may know the certainty of the things you have been taught. (Luke 1:1–4)

Likewise, John writes near the end of his gospel:

> Jesus did many other miraculous signs in the presence of his disciples, which are not recorded in this book. But these are written that you may believe that Jesus is the Christ, the Son of God, and that by believing you may have life in his name. (John 20:30–31)

Once you have examined the text, consult a good commentary for more discussion of this vital question. And then keep the reason for the book clearly in mind as you interpret its individual texts, always relating them to their larger purpose.

WHAT KIND OF LITERATURE IS THIS?

The Bible is composed of many different kinds of literature: history, law, poetry, letters, figures of speech, apocalyptic literature, etc. The way you would read poetry is not the way you would approach history. Let's look briefly at the different literary categories in God's word.[5]

History. (i.e., Genesis; Exodus 1–19; Numbers to Esther; portions of the prophets; Gospels; and Acts) should be read as factual narrative, seeking truths and principles within the events themselves. You should avoid attaching symbolic meaning to historical occurrences.

For example, the resurrection of Jesus Christ is a fact of history, not merely a symbol for renewed hope in the disciples.

Law. (i.e., Exodus 20–40; Leviticus) should be read to discover principles for living today, except where it is renewed in the New Testament and retains the force of law for Christian faith and practice.

Poetry. (i.e., Job to Song.) should be read symbolically, without pressing the details for historical accuracy or specific promises. For instance, the Psalmist states, "The Lord watches over you—the Lord is your shade at your right hand; the sun will not harm you by day, nor the moon by night" (Ps. 121:5–6). This poetry is obviously concerned with God's larger care for his own, not the specific problem of sunburn or exposure. Interpret poetry in terms of its intended symbols.

Letters. (i.e., parts of the Old Testament prophets; Romans to Jude) should always be read with their immediate audience and concerns in mind. You must not apply a letter's meaning to your situation until you are sure of the author's intended application to his audience.

Apocalyptic Literature. (i.e., parts of Zechariah, Ezekial and Daniel; Revelation) is highly visionary, and tends to be symbolic and future-oriented. The method you choose for interpreting these books will largely determine the meanings you find there.

It is important that you approach the book you are studying in a way which is consistent with its type of literature. Only then can you see the intended meaning of the text, which is the object of all Bible study. You may be surprised at how much this preliminary work will help you interpret your passage. Here you lay the foundation for all good Bible study.

CHECK YOURSELF 2

1. Match the term on the left with the definition on the right

    ____ Task theology   a. Read always with the immediate audience in mind

    ____ History   b. Unless renewed in the New Testament, should be read for principles

_____ Law

c. Highly visionary, tends to be symbolic and future-oriented

_____ Poetry

d. Literature written for a specific purpose

_____ Letters

e. Should be read symbolically

_____ Apocalyptic literature

f Should be read as factual narrative

STUDYING THE TEXT: THE "FOUR-FOLD" APPROACH

Now you can turn to a specific passage you want to study.

Read it three times, in three different translations (literal, dynamic equivalence, and free). Note what seems to be the major idea of the passage, and its relation to the author's purpose for the book.

At this preliminary point, ask these basic questions of the text:

• Who is speaking, writing, and/or acting?

• What is the subject of the text?

• When is this occurring?

• Where is it happening?

• Why and/or how?

It is very important that you have these answers firmly in mind. They will save you much confusion later.

Now we're ready to move into the heart of our Bible study method: the "four-fold approach." First, study the *grammar*—the words and sentences. Second, study the *history*—its geography and historical context. Third, study the *theology*—its central ideas and truths. Fourth, study the *practical*—how to apply these truths to life today. This basic method is the center of our "general hermeneutic"— our approach to the study of any passage in God's word.

GRAMMATICAL PRINCIPLES

Because we believe that the Bible can be understood, we will begin with the text itself—with its words and phrases. You should delay your interpretation and application until you know what the words of the text mean to say. The text itself is to be studied in stages.

Word Study ("lexicography"). We begin with the actual words of the passage. They must be studied carefully because we want to know what the author *intended* to say, not just what the word seems to say to us today. Words which survive long in any language acquire added meanings and implications. We must be sure we know the meaning of the word which its author intended.

For instance, Jesus told of a man who went on a journey and entrusted his servants with certain "talents" (Matt. 25:14–30). In our language "talent" means "gift" or "ability." But in Jesus' day a "talent" was a measure of money, worth more than a thousand dollars today. While this text may apply to the use of our abilities for God, it originally referred to the investment of money.

How can you do a word study? There are five important questions to answer. First, how was the word *defined?* You should define all important or unclear words in your text, with the help of a Bible dictionary. Be careful—confine your work to the definition of the word as it was intended by its original author.

Second, what is the *context* of the word? Often the immediate context will explain the meaning of a word or phrase. For example, Jesus referred to the "kingdom of God" in the Model Prayer (Matt. 6:10). What does the "kingdom" mean? Jesus defined it himself: "your kingdom come, your will be done on earth as it is in heaven." This is use of a kind of Hebrew poetry called "parallelism," where the second line repeats or defines the first. Thus the "kingdom" is where God's will is done. The context defines the term.

Third, what is the *history* of the word? A dictionary or encyclopedia will give you the background and root meanings of the word. Again, be careful to confine your study to meanings current when the author used the word. Also, work with the word in its original language, with the help of a dictionary or commentary. The history of its *translated* word may have nothing to do with the author's original intent.

For instance, Jesus begins each of His "beatitudes" with the phrase, "Blessed are . . . ." The English word "blessed" has an interesting history. It may be taken from the Old English word "bliss," meaning "joy." It may come from "blod," meaning "blood sacrifice"—something is "blessed" if it has been atoned for by sacrifice. It may come from "benedicere," meaning "to wish well." On this basis one might interpret the beatitudes: "How joyous and wished-well are those for whom Jesus has sacrificed His blood." All this may be in the background of "blessed."[6]

However, Jesus did *not* use our English word "blessed"—He used the Greek word "makarios." And it has none of this background in its history. "Makarios" describes a happiness which transcends circumstances, a joy beyond words or the world. So, study the history of the word, but make certain you are working with the word the author used and the way he used it.

Fourth, what are other biblical uses of the word? A concordance or dictionary will help here. Because Scripture interprets Scripture, other passages can often help clarify the meaning of the words of the text. For instance, remember that Jesus warns us that one who calls someone a "fool" is in danger of the "fire of hell" (Matt. 5:22). Why is calling someone a "fool" so terrible? As we have seen, in the Bible a "fool" is a person of the worst moral deficiency, one who rejects God and lives a life of terrible corruption. Consider Psalm 14:1: "The fool says in his heart, 'There is no God.' They are corrupt, their deeds are vile; there is no one who does good." And so to call someone a "fool" is to use the worst kind of insult. By comparing Scripture with Scripture, we can often clarify the words of the text at hand.

Fifth, what is the cultural background behind the word? What practices were current in the author's day which affected his use of the word? Remember Jesus' statement, "If someone forces you to go one mile, go with him two" (Matt. 5:41). What did Jesus mean by "forces you"? There was a well-known Persian custom, taken over by the Romans, by which a subject could be forced to carry a soldier's pack for one mile. This was more an act of slavery and oppression than a physical burden. Jesus is saying, If someone humiliates you, allow him to humiliate you even further. Treat even your enemies with humble service. The cultural background clarifies the word.

To summarize, you should begin your study of the actual text with its words. Define and clarify their meaning, with the help of a dictionary, concordance, encyclopedia, and/or commentary.

You must know the meaning of the words of God if you would interpret the word of God.

Sentence Structure. Often the grammar of the Hebrew, Aramaic, or Greek text will affect its meaning for us. It helps to know the sentence structure of any text you're studying. Here a good commentary is very helpful.

For an example of the importance of Hebrew sentence structure, consider Genesis 3:12: "The man said, 'The woman you put here with me—she gave me some of the fruit from the tree, and I ate it.'" Who is Adam blaming for his sin, the woman or the One who made her? The grammar answers the question.

The Hebrew words actually translate literally: "the woman / the man / and he said / with me / you gave / whom / the tree from / to me she gave / she / and I / ate." The use of the personal pronoun "she" in the Hebrew subjective case before the verb places focus on the one performing the action. Thus Adam is directly and emphatically blaming Eve for his sin. Don't be concerned—you do not need to know Hebrew grammar to understand this point, but you should use a commentary written by someone who does.

An important example of the significance of Greek sentence structure is 1 John 3:9. The King James translates this verse, "Whosoever is born of God doth not commit sin; for his seed remaineth in him: and he cannot sin, because he is born of God." The Greek verbs are in the "imperfect" tense, which means a continued action. Thus the NIV translates: "No one who is born of God will *continue* to sin, because God's seed remains in him; he cannot *go on* sinning, because he has been born of God" (emphasis mine).

Literary Type. We discussed earlier the importance of the kind of literature which comprises the book under investigation. However, the specific text should also be investigated in the same way. For instance, in the Gospel of Matthew, which is the "gospel" or "narrative" literature type, there are symbols, teaching discourses, and apocalyptic sections. You must be careful to determine the literary type of your specific text also.

Each of the guidelines discussed in this section will also help with passages within the biblical books. In addition to these, you should consider another literary device which will often affect a passage: the *figure of speech.* This is a common, powerful communication tool. One biblical figure of speech is the "metaphor," an illustration using a direct comparison which is not intended to be taken literally. For instance, Jesus says, "I am the true vine" (John 15:1), clearly a metaphorical statement. Another figure of speech is the "simile," a comparison using "like" or "as." For example, "the sight of the glory of the Lord was like devouring fire" (Ex. 24:17, KJV) is a simile. A third is the "hyperbole," a statement which uses exaggeration to make a point. Again, it is not intended to be read literally. For instance, Jesus says, "if your right eye causes you to sin, gouge it out and throw it away" (Matt. 5:29). Here it is vital that you interpret the text as Jesus intends!

Context. One last step in "grammatical" interpretation involves considering the larger context of the passage in question. Three questions should be asked. First, what is the general idea of the larger passage where the text is found? Second, how does the text contribute to the flow of the author's thought in the larger chapter and book?

Third, is this passage teaching "prescriptive" or "descriptive" truth? Prescriptive statements are intended as commands for the reader. For instance, "Do not judge, or you too will be judged" (Matt. 7:1) prescribes behavior for all readers. Descriptive statements simply describe the event, without endorsing it as proper then or now. For instance, 1 Kings 11:3 states that Solomon had seven hundred wives and three hundred concubines. This description does not prescribe this behavior for us.

It will help to think in "contextual circles" in studying the text[7] (see Figure 7.1). Begin with the immediate verses, then study their context in the chapter, then the section of the book, then the book, then the Testament, then the Bible. You may be surprised at how this study clarifies the application of the specific text today.

Note: the smaller the quantity of material to be interpreted, the greater is the danger of ignoring its context. Heed the proverb: "a text without a context is only a pretext." Make sure you understand the text in its larger setting and purpose.

Summary. Grammatical Bible study requires the following:

1. Study the words in the passage; see their definition, context, history, other biblical uses, and cultural background.

2. Understand the sentence structure.

3. Define the literary type of the text.

4. Know its place in the larger context of God's word.

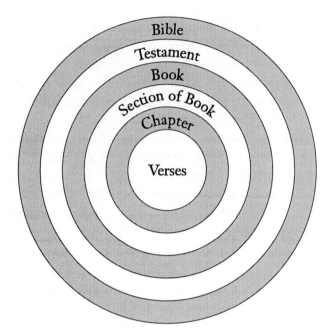

Figure 7.1 Contextual circles

Martin Luther said, "At its root, all theology is grammar." So is all Bible study. The study of God's words is indispensable to the understanding of His word.

Historical Principles

The second major part of our "four-fold approach" concerns the historical background of the text. While you have already investigated the history behind some of the words of the passage, now it helps to understand historical considerations related to the passage itself. Two major areas are important here.

Geography. Often the location of biblical places has a direct bearing on the interpretation of associated texts. In addition, the more you know about the land where the biblical events took place, the better you will feel you understand the events and their significance. For these reasons it is a good investment of your time to familiarize yourself with the basic layout of the biblical lands. A good atlas or map will help you here. In addition, you should know the geography behind any specific text you are seeking to study. Two examples demonstrate the importance of geography.

First, consider Jeremiah 13:1–5:

This is what the Lord said to me: "Go and buy a linen belt and put it around your waist, but do not let it touch water." So I bought a belt, as the Lord directed, and put it around my waist. Then the word of the Lord came to me a second time: "Take the belt you bought and are wearing around your waist, and go now to Perath and hide it there in a crevice in the rocks." So I went and hid it at Perath, as the Lord told me.

This seems a rather routine text, until we learn that Perath lay 430 miles from where Jeremiah received this command. The long, arduous, and dangerous trip described points up the sacrifice often necessary to obedience.

Second, remember Luke 2:4: "So Joseph also went up from the town of Nazareth in Galilee to Judea, to Bethlehem the town of David." This was a journey of some ninety miles, made on a donkey's back by a woman who was heavy with child. Fulfilling God's promise that Messiah would be born in Bethlehem (Micah 5:2) required great sacrifice for His mother. The geography of the text makes it seem alive and relevant.

Social Context. Often knowledge of the customs or general historical situation greatly illuminates the biblical text.

First, consider material objects. For instance, Matthew 27:34 says "There [on the cross] they offered [Jesus] wine to drink, mixed with gall; but after tasting it, He refused to drink it."

However, John 19:28–30 describes Jesus' requesting and drinking wine on the cross. This seems to be a confusing contradiction until we study the wines themselves. The drink Matthew refers to was a kind of narcotic customarily given to crucifixion victims to dull their senses. Jesus refused this anesthetic, choosing to be fully awake and alert. John's reference occurred six hours later, when Jesus requested and received a mild vinegar-wine to moisten His lips and make possible His final words from the cross. Studying the objects in question clears up the confusion.

Second, study social customs—practices or rites which society observed in biblical times. For example, Jesus' speaking to the Samaritan woman at Sychar shocked even her: "You are a Jew and I am a Samaritan woman. How can you ask me for a drink?" (John 4:9). This question makes sense when we learn that the Jews hated the Samaritans, and that Jewish rabbis often would not speak to any woman in public during the day. Jesus thus broke with popular prejudice in winning this woman to Himself. Often we must do the same today.

Third, investigate historical facts. Often basic facts of life in the biblical period are presupposed by the writer but unknown to readers today.

For example, Jesus said in Matt. 25:1–3,

> At that time the kingdom of heaven will be like ten virgins who took their lamps and went out to meet the bridegroom. Five of them were foolish and five were wise. The foolish ones took their lamps but did not take any oil with them.

What made these women so foolish? As any of Matthew's original readers would have known, ancient oil lamps were made very small so that three or four could be held in the hand at once. Not to take more oil was very foolish, as a marriage vigil could last as long as three hours and so exhaust the supply of oil in the little lamps. The foolish virgins were not condemned for their inability to predict the time of the groom's return (Jesus' second coming), but for their lack of readiness in the things they knew to be doing. From the historical facts behind the text, we discover its application for our lives today.

SUMMARY: HISTORICAL BIBLE STUDY REQUIRES THE FOLLOWING:

1. Know the people or peoples who are involved in the text.

2. Know the time-frame of the events of the passage.

3. Check the place or places which provide the geographical setting, and any significance of this setting for the meaning of the passage.

4. Note the customs, culture, or other historical facts present in the text.

5. Especially be aware of differences and similarities between the original situation and ours today. Otherwise, the intended meaning will likely be lost on the contemporary reader.

A well-known example of differences between the biblical situation and ours is the parable of the Good Samaritan. It is commonplace today to speak of one who does a good deed as a "Good Samaritan," but this phrase would have been an oxymoron and a scandal to Jesus' first audience. The Samaritans were descended from those Jews who remained in Palestine during the Babylonian exile, many of whom intermarried with other races. The Jews who returned from Babylon considered the Samaritans half-breeds, and despised them. For a Samaritan to help a wounded Jew after a priest and Levite had refused him would be similar to a black man in the 1960s helping an injured white man after his pastor and deacon had left him for dead. You must communicate accurately the actual historical situation, and then the text demonstrates its relevance clearly.

Once you are familiar with the author's purpose for his book and this text, you know the meaning of his words and phrases, and you are familiar with the historical and social background of the passage, you are ready to interpret the text theologically and practically. You have laid the foundation for an excellent application of God's word today.

THEOLOGICAL PRINCIPLES

The third major part of our "four-fold approach" deals with theological principles contained in the passage. Here it is important to study two main areas.

Scripture interprets Scripture. Now that you have developed the grammatical-historical meaning of the text, relate that meaning to the rest of God's word. Using a topical Bible or concordance, see what other passages say on this subject. But be careful: never take any other passage out of its context to make it fit your study here. Only relate those texts which are intended by their author for this application.

General Theological Concepts. Now apply the meaning of the text to general theological questions. For example, see what the passage says about:

- God
- Humanity
- Creation and the world

- Sin

- Salvation

- Missions

- The future

What other theological significance is found within the text? What key theological contributions does the passage make today?

Let's assume you are studying Matthew 5:13: "You are the salt of the earth. But if the salt loses its saltiness, how can it be made salty again? It is no longer good for anything, except to be thrown out and trampled by men." In studying the grammar and history of the text, you have learned that salt was a common preservative in Jesus' day. Theologically, Jesus is therefore saying that His disciples are essential to His saving work on earth. As we fulfill our mission, we help preserve the world from judgment through salvation. But if we lose our "saltiness" and become like our fallen world, we lose our purpose in life. Our evangelistic mission, seeking to share Christ with a lost humanity, is God's purpose for us. This theological fact is of great significance for the church in our secular day.

The theological principles suggested by a text are especially important to the passage's relevance today. However, these principles *must* be grounded in the author's intended meaning, as discovered by grammatical-historical study. This is why our "four-fold method" builds theological application upon textual investigation. One should never reverse the order.

PRACTICAL PRINCIPLES

The last area in our "four-fold approach" concerns practical applications of the text. Because human nature does not change, biblical truth is always relevant and must be applied personally and practically.

Dwight Moody spoke to the relevance of the Bible in this way:

A great many people seem to think that the Bible is out of date, that it is an old book, and they think it has passed its day. They say it was a very good book for the Dark Ages, and that there is some very good history in it. But then it was not intended for the present time; we are living in a very enlightened age, and that men can get on very well without the old book, that we have outgrown it. They think we have no use for it, because it is an old book.

Now you might just as well say that the sun, which has shone so long, is now so old that it is out of date, and that whenever a man builds a house he need not put any windows on it, because we have a newer light and a better light; we have gas-light and this new electric light. These are something new; and I would advise people, if they think the Bible is too old and worn out, when they build houses, not to put any windows in them, but just to light them with this new electric light. That is something new, and this is what they are anxious for.[8]

The Bible was given to be applied to daily life. If you do not seek the practical application of the text, you have not completed its study and interpretation. Your objective should be to reproduce the original meaning of the text in today's culture.

There are five steps in applying the text practically:

Write out the intended meaning of the text. On the basis of your grammatical-historical study, define the meaning and purpose of the text for its author and original readers.

Note differences in setting and context. In your historical investigation, you will have observed changes in culture and context from the text to our day, some of which will significantly affect its contemporary application (i.e., the "Good Samaritan" story).

Make direct applications where intended by the author. Where the writer's intended purpose and meaning "transfers" directly to our culture and needs, make this application as practically as is appropriate. For instance, Jesus' statement, "You are the salt of the earth" (Matt. 5:13) is a "prescriptive" truth which applies as directly to us as it did to His first disciples. Make this application, pointing out its practical consequences today.

Seek principles within the passage when the text does not apply directly to our day. Where the text is a law which is not renewed in the New Testament (such as a dietary code) or a historical event which does not "prescribe" a specific application (such as the Battle of Jericho), do not apply the text directly as if it were prescriptive. Otherwise, all Christians would be forced to follow outdated dietary laws, and warfare would be reduced to marching around enemy walls. Rather, seek *principles* within the text which apply to today's needs, keeping these principles consistent with the author's intended meaning.

For instance, dietary laws reveal the practical principle that God cares deeply about our bodies and health. The Battle of Jericho shows that God's will, when obeyed, always leads to the victory He promises. You should find such general principles within the author's intended purpose and apply them practically.

The use of principles is often the best way to approach culture-bound biblical statements. For example, "Greet one another with a holy kiss" is a common command in Paul's letters (Rom. 16:16; 1 Cor. 16:20; 2 Cor. 13:12; 1 Thess. 5:26). The meaning of the words and grammar are just as the verses read. But in Paul's society persons often greeted one another publicly with a kiss, unlike our culture today. In our context, these verses suggest the principle that Christians should greet one another with great kindness and love, whether this is by word, hand, or other physical expression. We are commanded to obey the *principle* of the text.

Likewise, commands to individuals in the Bible are not always commands to us today. Abraham was commanded to offer Isaac (Gen. 22); this prescription is not incumbent on fathers today. We need to apply the principle of the text—as a father, even my sons must be dedicated to God and His will. Bernard Ramm comments:

> *The Bible is more a book of principles than a catalogue of specific directions.* The Bible does contain an excellent blend of the general and the specific with reference to principles for Christian living. If the Bible were never specific we would be somewhat disconcerted in attempting a specific application of its principles. If the Bible were entirely specific in its principles, we would be adrift whenever confronted with a situation in life not covered by a specific principle. The *emphasis* in Scripture is on moral and spiritual principles, not upon specific and itemized lists of rules for moral or spiritual conduct.[9]

By discovering practical principles within the author's intended meaning, you will find that every passage in the Bible possesses personal relevance today.

Define at least one action which the text suggests today. When you have finished your study of the text, you should be able to describe at least one practical action which you will take as a result of the author's intended purpose. Then you can determine ways to communicate this application to others.

Mark Twain once said, "When I read the Bible, the parts that trouble me the most are not the ones I don't understand, but the ones I do understand."[10] You should have a sense of conviction and direction every time you interpret God's word.

For instance, when you have finished your study of Matthew 5:13 you should be able to describe at least one practical way you can act as a "preservative" in your fallen world today. You might resolve to share the gospel with a lost friend, or to pray specifically for a mission cause or person. There should be at least one practical result of your work any time you study the word of God.

CHECK YOURSELF 3

Rather than testing your recall of specific terms and facts discussed here, work to familiarize yourself with the "four-fold method" in outline form:

I. *Grammatical principles*—discover the meaning of the words and sentences in the text
   A. Word study—what are the words intended to say?
      1. How was the word defined?
      2. What is its context?
      3. What is its history?
      4. What are other biblical uses of the word?
      5. What is the cultural background of the word?
   B. Sentence structure—how does the grammar of the text help to understand its meaning?
   C. Literary type—what kind of literature is found in the text?
   D. Context—what is the place of the text in its larger passage?
      1. What is the general idea of the larger passage?
      2. How does the text contribute to the author's thought in this larger passage?
      3. Is the text in its context teaching a truth or describing an event?

II. *Historical principles*—discover the significance of historical factors behind the text
   A.

Geography—how does the locale of places and people in the text help to understand its meaning?

B. Social context—what customs are important to understanding the passage?
1. What is the meaning of material objects mentioned?
2. How do social customs affect the meaning?
3. What historical facts are of importance?

III. *Theological principles*—discover theological truths and applications within the text
A. Scripture interprets Scripture—how do other passages clarify the meaning and application of this text?
B. General theological concepts—what does the passage say about such subjects as God, man, creation, sin, salvation, mission, and the future?

IV. *Practical principles*—discover the relevant applications of the text to lives and issues today.
A. Write out the intended meaning of the text.
B. Note differences in setting and context.
C. Make direct applications where they are intended by the author.
D. Seek principles within the passage where the text does not apply directly to our day.
E. Define at least one action which the text suggests today.

These principles are basic to all Bible study, and will help you get more from any part of God's word.

Other Methods of Bible Study

We'll close by surveying briefly other methods of Bible study. In addition to the verse-by-verse approach discussed above, at least six other approaches to Bible study are also popular and helpful today.[11]

Topical Study

This consists of defining a topic and researching the Bible to see what it says on the subject. For instance, in studying Matthew 5:13, you might want to know more about the biblical topic of "earth."

Define the topic carefully. Instead of beginning with every reference in the Bible to the earth, limit your research to its intended meaning here—the physical world.

Consult a dictionary or encyclopedia for an overview of the subject.

List other topics which relate to this one (i.e., "world," "creation").

Organize your research in contextual circles: the "earth" in the Sermon on the Mount, in the Gospel of Matthew, in the teaching of Jesus, in the New Testament, in the Bible. Realize that the farther you move from the first circles, the greater the chance that references may not relate to the original passage's intended meaning.

List personal, practical conclusions from each relevant text, and an overall summary thesis. Topical studies can be very helpful and relevant, so long as they are always based on the author's intended purpose for the different texts studied.

Biographical Study

Here you would gather together the different biblical texts regarding a specific figure.

Decide on your subject. Be careful—the more important the person in the Bible, the more involved your study will be.

List passages in chronological order, and summarize your findings. A concordance or encyclopedia article will help here.

Write out conclusions: life, actions, personality, strengths, weaknesses, things to emulate, things to avoid, principles for life today.

Word-Study

Choose a subject for study (i.e., "light of the world", Matt. 5:14). Be careful—one Hebrew, Aramaic, or Greek word can be translated several different ways in English. Likewise, one English word can render several different words in the original languages. Consult commentaries along the way regarding the different texts you study.

Limit your study—look at "light" in the teaching of Jesus, for instance.

Use a concordance to locate references, in contextual circles.

Record conclusions: for example, the meaning of the word or phrase, its various uses, ways its meaning changes in the Bible, and personal and practical applications today.

Bible Themes and Doctrines

Define a subject (i.e., "we should let our light shine before men," Matt. 5:16).

Consult a topical Bible and/or concordance for texts, in contextual circles.

Summarize the finding of each appropriate passage. Again, confine interpretation to authorial intent and purpose.

Organize your findings into a systematic presentation. You would seek to know how the different texts relate and present a unified doctrine.

Note practical, contemporary applications.

Question and Answer

Define a subject (i.e., "how do people 'hide their light' today?" Matt. 5:14–15).

Define the subjects to investigate: light, witnessing, ineffective witness.

Do word studies (see "word-study" above).

Summarize findings and applications.

Book Study

Decide on your subject (i.e, the Gospel of Matthew)

Answer introductory questions: author, place, purpose, recipients, time-frame, historical concerns.

Read the book in one setting, noting its major theme and outlining its main ideas. Then revise these with the help of a commentary introduction to the book.

Break down major ideas into sub-points and key verses. Define ways these help accomplish the author's intended purpose for his book.

Describe ways the book contributes to the larger purpose of the Bible; i.e., how does Matthew's Gospel help us know Christ and spread His Kingdom?

Note applications of the major theme and from each part of the book for life today.

Conclusion

As we stated at the outset, this is the most practical chapter in our study. The precepts set forth here apply to your study of every text in God's word. By work and practice, you will soon be able to use these principles with skill and confidence.

Throughout your practice of these study methods, keep in mind their purpose. They are a means to an end, intended to help you get more from God's word so that you might better know the Lord Himself. J. W. Alexander once observed, "The study of God's word, for the purpose of discovering God's will, is the secret discipline which has formed the greatest characters."[12] May these principles be used by God to form the character of Christ in you.

Answers

Check Yourself 1

1. do not   2. New, Old   3. later, earlier   4. unclear, clear   5. Brief, longer   6. for all time   7. both

Check Yourself 2

1. d, f, b, e, a, c

Conclusion

A LIFETIME OF LIFE-CHANGING BIBLE STUDY

I spent the summer before my senior year of college as a missionary in East Malaysia, in Southeast Asia. The country is officially Muslim and allows no open evangelism of the Malay people. As a result, Bibles are not available to much of the country's population.

We were able to bring a few paperback Malay-language Bibles with us across the border. I will never forget the service where we gave them out. An elderly woman came to the front of the church, her wrinkled and spotted hands trembling, tears of joy sparkling on her weathered cheeks. She took my little paperback Bible in her hands, cradled it reverently, and then held it to her heart, eyes closed in prayer. I thought of all my Bibles at home on the shelf, gathering dust. And I asked God to forgive my complacency with His word.

The Bible is meant to be read and obeyed. God intends His word to change your life. And it will, given the chance.

Listen to this letter to the editor of a Russian magazine. The writer expresses anger that it wasn't until at age thirty that he was allowed to read the Gospels, and says,

> This miniature book reached me quite by accident, and I approached it purely out of literary curiosity. But the text gripped me: I was impressed by the severe power of the words, the elegance of the finely tuned aphorisms, the subtle poetic quality of the images. I became clear [sic] that the esthetic importance of the volume was indisputable, and gradually I became very angry: What a treasure they have been hiding from me! Who decided, and on what basis, that this was bad for me—and why?[1]

God's word *is* powerful and life-changing. Now let us see how *you* can experience its power more personally. After looking over what we have studied so far, we will close with suggestions for a lifetime of personal Bible study.

THE PRACTICE OF DAILY BIBLE STUDY

Consider the following facts about the Bible: the King James Version has 3,566,480 letters, 733,746 words, 31,163 verses, and 1,189 chapters. The longest chapter in the Bible is the 119th Psalm; the shortest is the 117th Psalm; and the middle verse of the Bible is Psalm 118:8. The longest word in the Bible is found in Isaiah 8:1,3—"Mahershalalhashbaz".

The longest verse is Esther 8:9; the shortest is John 11:35. And every letter of the alphabet is found in Ezra 7:21 (KJV). So what? That's exactly the question.

Learning *about* the Bible is not really the point—what we need is to know God personally through His word. Our study to this point will help you better know about the word of God. But now it is up to you to meet God there. Daily Bible study is vital to daily spiritual growth. Every Christian needs a time each day to be with God in His word.

Years ago, the great violinist Yehudi Menuhin when at the very height of international fame, took an absence of two years from the concert stage. Here's his explanation:

> One of the dangers which besets all artists is staleness. I simply wanted to do the best for myself and for my audience. That is why I retired

for two years, to remain for a while alone—just me and my Stradivarius.[2]

How much more I need "a while alone," just me and God in His word. A recent Gallup Poll showed that while 82 percent of Americans believe the Bible is either the "literal" or "inspired" word of God, only 21 percent are engaged in Bible study.

Obviously, many of us need more time in God's word. What are some good ways to develop or strengthen daily Bible study? Reading schedules can help, as can a daily routine.

READING SCHEDULES

There are any number of ways to read the Bible regularly. "Through the Bible in a Year" programs are to be found in the back of most study Bibles and devotional guides. In addition to these, the following have been most helpful to me.

A One-month New Testament Plan. The first suggestion is a plan for reading through the New Testament in a month. This kind of intensive program has given me a good overview of the New Testament in its larger themes and doctrines. Follow this schedule for three months, reading in three different translations (see chap. 5 for translation suggestions).[3] Here's the schedule:

Matthew 1–9	Acts 21–28
Matthew 10–17	Romans 1–6
Matthew 18–24	Romans 7–16
Matthew 25—Mark 4	1 Corinthians 1–9
Mark 5–10	1 Corinthians 10–16
Mark 11–16	2 Corinthians
Luke 1–6	Galatians, Ephesians
Luke 7–11	Philippians, Colossians,
Luke 12–18	and 1 Thessalonians
Luke 19–24	2 Thessalonians, 1 and 2 Timothy
John 1–7	Titus, Philemon, Hebrews 1–9
John 8–14	Hebrews 10–13, James
John 15–21	1, 2 Peter, 1–3 John
Acts 1–7	Jude, Revelation 1–11
Acts 8–14	Revelation 12–22
Acts 15–20	

Notice that you will not read the same number of chapters each day. The schedule is designed for you to read approximately the same number of pages daily, given the varying lengths of different chapters.

A Three-month New Testament Plan. A second model preserves the same overview approach as the first but requires less daily reading. This schedule has been helpful to many in developing Bible study discipline.

Month 1	*Month 2*	*Month 3*
1. Matthew 1–3	1. John 1–2	1. 1 Corinthians 10–11
2. Matthew 4–6	2. John 3–4	2. 1 Corinthians 12–13
3. Matthew 7–9	3. John 5–7	3. 1 Corinthians 14–16
4. Matthew 10–12	4. John 8–10	4. 2 Corinthians 1–4
5. Matthew 13–15	5. John 11–12	5. 2 Corinthians 5–8
6. Matthew 16–17	6. John 13–14	6. 2 Corinthians 9–13
7. Matthew 18–20	7. John 15–16	7. Galatians 1–4
8. Matthew 21–22	8. John 17–18	8. Galatians 5–6, Ephesians 1–2
9. Matthew 23–24	9. Acts 1	9. Ephesians 3–6
10. Matthew 25–27	10. Acts 2	10. Philippians
11. Matthew 28– Mark 1	11. Acts 3–5	11. Colossians
12. Mark 2–4	12. Acts 6–7	12. 1 Thessalonians
13. Mark 5–6	13. Acts 8–10	13. 2 Thessalonians
14. Mark 7–8	14. Acts 11–12	14. 1 Timothy
15. Mark 9–10	15. Acts 13–14	15. 2 Timothy
16. Mark 11–12	16. Acts 15–16	16. Titus
17. Mark 13–14	17. Acts 17–18	17. Philemon, Hebrews 1–4
18. Mark 15–16	18. Acts 19–20	18. Hebrews 5–9
19. Luke 1–2	19. Acts 21–23	19. Hebrews 10–13
20. Luke 3–4	20. Acts 24–26	20. James 1–2
21. Luke 5–6	21. Acts 27–28	21. James 3–5
22. Luke 7–8	22. Romans 1–2	22. 1 Peter
23. Luke 9–10	23. Romans 3–4	23. 2 Peter, 1 John
24. Luke 11	24. Romans 5–7	24. 2, 3 John
25. Luke 12–13	25. Romans 8–10	25. Jude, Revelation 1–3
26. Luke 14–16	26. Romans 11–13	26. Revelation 4–7
27. Luke 17–18	27. Romans 14–16	27. Revelation 8–11
28. Luke 19–20	28. 1 Corinthians 1–3	28. Revelation 12–15
29. Luke 21–22	29. 1 Corinthians 4–6	29. Revelation 16–19
30. Luke 23–24	30. 1 Corinthians 7–9	30. Revelation 20–22

An Annual Bible Reading Plan. The plan I am following right now takes me through the Bible each year. It's an old method, but it keeps me on track each morning. The plan is to read two chapters in the Old Testament and one in the New Testament each day. For the Old Testament, begin at Genesis 1 and Ezra 1; for the New Testament, begin at Matthew 1. At the end of the year, depending on the yearly calendar and your own discipline, you will be close to finishing the entire Bible. This approach has been followed through the years by many people, and it helps me gain a holistic view of God's word each year.

Undoubtedly other plans could be just as helpful. The point is to find a method and stay with it. You will find your time invested each day in God's word to be indispensable in your spiritual growth.

A SUGGESTED ROUTINE

You not only need a plan for daily Bible reading—you also need a routine and time commitment. The actual time needed to read the Bible through each year is far less than most people think. In fact, it has been calculated that it takes seventy hours and forty minutes to read the Bible at the average speaking rate—fifty-two hours and twenty minutes for the Old Testament and eighteen hours and twenty minutes for the New Testament. This is less than twelve minutes a day—surely time well spent!

There are many ways to schedule a daily time with God in His word. My suggestion is that you do this the first thing in the morning. It was Jesus' pattern to rise early to be with God (Mark 1:35), and other key figures followed the same method as well (see Jacob in Gen. 28:16–18; Samuel's parents in 1 Sam. 1:19; Hezekiah in 2 Chron. 29:20; Job in Job 1:5; and David in Psalm 57:8). Set a time each day to read God's word and pray. Work your schedule around your time with God—make this time your first priority in the day.

It also helps to set a place to read and pray each day. The more you can establish a routine, the more habitual your time with God will be. In addition, I strongly urge you to create a "spiritual notebook." This can be one of several such notebooks currently available in Christian bookstores, or you can make your own. Use this to take notes from your daily Bible reading, especially practical applications for the day. Your notebook is also a good place for daily prayer lists and a spiritual journal. I have found my notebook to be the single most important tool in my daily spiritual growth.

Along with your planned Bible study, it is very helpful to find a key verse or text to memorize and meditate on for each day or week. Spurgeon said, "I would rather lay my soul asoak in half a dozen verses all day than rinse my hand in several chapters.[4]

In these ways your spirit is in touch daily with God in His word.

AN APPEAL

When Karl Marx was seventeen years old, he wrote an excellent study of part of the Gospel of John. Many theologians agree with much of what Marx wrote. Eventually, of course, he rejected the Bible and during his adult life called himself an atheist.

Likewise, Nikita Krushchev, the former premier of the USSR, read the Bible when he was a boy. But when he became an adult, he made it his ambition to bury the church in the Soviet Union by 1965.[5] Clearly, just reading the Bible, even on a daily schedule, is not enough.

This book is about the Bible. I hope that you have learned more about the Scriptures. But what really matters is not to learn *about* God's word, but to learn *from* it.

Only when you apply God's word personally to your daily life does it accomplish its intended purpose for you. An old rabbi was walking down the village street. A member of his synagogue walked up to him, boasting loudly that he had read through all the volumes of the Talmud three times. The rabbi replied, "The important thing is not how many times you have been through the Talmud, but whether the Talmud has been through you."[6] Likewise, the Buddhists have a saying, "To know and not to use is not yet to know." Let us make the prayer of Thomas a Kempis our own: "Let not thy Word, O Lord, become a judgment on us, That we hear it and do it not, That we know it and love it not, That we believe it and obey it not."[7]

J. I. Packer is right—the Bible is God preaching. And His sermons are to be applied. Scripture is to be obeyed, practically and personally. To unlock God's word, the most important key of all is the one to your own heart.

NOTES

CHAPTER I

1. *National and International Report,* 4 May 1992, 1.

2. *Preaching* (September–October 1990): 45.

3. Newsbriefs, *Impact* (June 1991): 3.

4. Mortimer J. Adler and Charles van Doren, *How to Read a Book,* rev. ed. (New York: Simon and Schuster, A Touchstone Book, 1972), 60.

5. For more on these terms and their ancient uses, see Frank Stagg, *New Testament Theology* (Nashville: Broadman, 1962), 1.

6. Euripides, Andromache, *Great Books of the Western World,* 2d ed., ed. Mortimer J. Adler, no. 4 (Chicago: Encyclopaedia Britannica, Inc., 1990), 449.

7. See C. F. H. Henry, *God, Revelation and Authority,* vol. 4 (Waco: Word, 1979),4:68.

8. For more reading on the subject of evidences for the Bible, consult the following. For a general overview, see Clark H. Pinnock, *Reason Enough: A Case for the Christian Faith* (Downers Grove, Ill.: InterVarsity Press, 1980); Pinnock, *Set Forth Your Case: An Examination of Christianity's Credentials* (Chicago: Moody, 1967); and the classic, Bernard Ramm, *Protestant Christian Evidences* (Chicago, Ill.: Moody, 1953). For bibliographic study: F. F. Bruce, *The New Testament Documents: Are They Reliable?* 5th ed., rev. (Downers Grove, Ill.: InterVarsity Press, 1960), 10–20; and Bruce M. Metzger, *The Text of the New Testament: Its Transmission, Corruption, and Restoration* (New York: Oxford University Press, 1964), 36–92. For archaeological evidences: John Arthur Thompson, *The Bible and Archaeology,* 3d ed., rev. (Grand Rapids, Mich.: Eerdmans, 1982). For prophecy study: Ramm, 81–124. For internal consistency, consult R. T. France, *The Evidence for Jesus* (Downers Grove, Ill.:

InterVarsity, 1986), 111–17. For personal experience: the classic text is E. Y. Mullins, *Why Is Christianity True?* 2d ed. (Chicago, Ill.: Winona Publishing Co., 1905).

9. "News Digest," *Time*, Aug. 16, 1993, 19. _See also Edgar V. McKnight, *Opening the Bible: A Guide to Understanding the Scriptures* (Nashville: Broadman Press, 1967), 121.

10. This approach was suggested by John R. W. Stott, *Culture and the Bible* (Downers Grove, Ill.: InterVarsity Press, 1979), 9–13.

11. A. H. Strong, *Systematic Theology* (Valley Forge, Pa.: Judson Press, 1907), 216.

12. In Veronica Zundel, comp. *Eerdmans' Book of Famous Prayers* (Grand Rapids, Mich.: Eerdmans, 1983), 47.

13. Southern Baptists have made an especially clear statement of this important truth by declaring that the Bible is "the supreme standard by which all human conduct, creeds, and religious opinions should be tried." See Herschel H. Hobbs, *The Baptist Faith and Message* (Nashville, Tenn.: Convention Press, 1971), 18.

14. Stott, 3.

15. From the preface to his New Testament; quoted in *Preaching* (May–June 1990): 16.

CHAPTER 2

1. William Barclay, *A Spiritual Autobiography* (Grand Rapids, Mich.: Eerdmans, 1975), 90.

2. See F. F. Bruce, *The New Testament Documents: Are They Reliable?* 5th rev. ed. (Downers Grove, Ill.: InterVarsity Press, 1977 [1960]), 16.

3. Ibid., 19–20.

4. Frederic Kenyon, *The Bible and Archaeology* (New York: Harper and Brothers, 1940), 288–89; quoted by Bruce, 20; emphasis his.

5. Among the many treatments of this subject, the following are especially recommended: F. F. Bruce, *The Canon of Scripture* (Downers Grove, Ill.: InterVarsity Press, 1988); Bruce M. Metzger, *The Canon of the New Testament: Its Origins, Development, and Significance* (Oxford: The Clarendon Press, 1987); and Lee Martin McDonald, *The Formation of the Christian Biblical Canon* (Nashville: Abingdon, 1988).

6. *Flavius Josephus Against Apion*, I:1.8. In *Josephus: Complete Works*, trans. William Whiston (Grand Rapids, Mich.: Kregel Publications, 1978 [1960]).

7. Justin, *The First Apology of Justin*, ch. 67, in *The Ante-Nicene Fathers*, ed. Alexander Roberts and James Donaldson, rev. A. Cleveland Coxe, 1:186 (Grand Rapids, Mich.: Eerdmans, reprinted 1989).

8. For more on this section, see William Barclay, *The Making of the Bible* (Edinburgh: The Saint Andrew Press, 1991 [1961]), 41–51.

9. Irenaeus (born ca. A.D. 130): "After their departure [the death of Peter and Paul], Mark, the disciple and interpreter of Peter, did also hand down to us in writing what had been preached by Peter. Luke also, the companion of Paul, recorded in a book the Gospel preached by him." See Irenaeus, *Against Heresies* III:1.1, in *The Ante-Nicene Fathers* 1:414.

10. *The First Epistle of Clement to the Corinthians*, 12, in *Ante-Nicene Fathers* I:12.

11. Clement of Rome (d. A.D. 97) made this point for his church:

> The apostles have preached the Gospel to us from the Lord Jesus Christ; Jesus Christ from God. Christ therefore was sent forth by God, and the apostles by

Christ. Both these appointments, then, were made in an orderly way, according to the will of God. Having therefore received their orders, and being fully assured by the resurrection of our Lord Jesus Christ, and established in the word of God, with full assurance of the Holy Ghost, they went forth proclaiming that the kingdom of God was at hand" (*First Clement*, 42 [*Ante-Nicene Fathers* 1:16])

12. The actual list and order of the Muratorian Canon was: Matthew, Mark, Luke, John, Acts, 1 and 2 Corinthians, Ephesians, Philippians, Colossians, Galatians, 1 and 2 Thessalonians, Romans, Philemon, Titus, 1 and 2 Timothy, Jude, 1 and 2 John, Revelation and the "Apocalypse of Peter" (a book excluded by most other lists and from our New Testament today).

13. Athanasius, *A Select Library of Nicene and Post-Nicene Fathers of the Christian Church* (Grand Rapids, Mich.: Eerdmans, repr. 1991), IV:552.

14. Bruce, *New Testament Documents*, 27.

15. Barclay, *Making of the Bible*, x.

CHAPTER 3

1. Most of the following are taken from John P. Newport and WilliamCannon, *Why Christians Fight Over the Bible* (Nashville: Thomas Nelson, 1974), 163–65.

2. For a larger discussion of these, see Henry A. Virkler, *Hermeneutics: Principles and Processes of Biblical Interpretation* (Grand Rapids, Mich.: Baker, 1981), 19–20.

3. Paul Ricoeur has stated well this need to cross history in studying the Bible:

There has always been a hermeneutical problem in Christianity because Christianity proceeds from a proclamation. It begins with a fundamental preaching that maintains that in Jesus Christ the kingdom has approached us in a decisive fashion. But this fundamental preaching, this word, comes to us through writings, through the Scriptures, and these must constantly be restored as the living word if the primitive word that witnessed to the fundamental and founding event is to remain contemporary (*Essays on Biblical Interpretation*, ed. with intro. by Lewis S. Mudge [Philadelphia: Fortress Press, 1980], 49).

4. Quoted in *Parables, Etc.* (Platteville, CO: Saratoga Press, September, 1990), 1.

CHAPTER 4

1. Conyers, 61; emphasis his.

2. See Yandall Woodfin, *With All Your Mind: A Christian Philosophy* (Nashville: Abingdon, 1980), 32–34.

3. The idea of the Bible as an hourglass is taken from McKnight, 43–44; the applications are mine.

4. James S. Stewart, *The Life and Teaching of Jesus Christ* (Nashville: Abingdon, n.d.), 47.

5. George Eldon Ladd, *The Presence of the Future: The Eschatology of Biblical Realism* (Grand Rapids, Mich.: Eerdmans, 1974), 45.

6. G. R. Beasley-Murray, *Jesus and the Kingdom of God* (Grand Rapids, Mich.: Eerdmans, 1986), 17, quoting Eissfeldt favorably.

7. Beasley-Murray, 22–24.

8. For an excellent survey of themes relating to Jesus and the Kingdom, consult Ladd, 149-339. For in-depth study of Jesus' own teachings on the subject of the Kingdom, see Beasley-Murray, 71-337.

9. George Eldon Ladd's excellent definition of the kingdom summarizes well our discussion:

The Kingdom of God is the redemptive reign of God dynamically active to establish his rule among men, and . . . this Kingdom, which will appear as an apocalyptic act at the end of the age, has already come into human history in the person and mission of Jesus to overcome evil, to deliver men from its power, and to bring them into the blessings of God's reign (Ladd, 218).

10. Conyers, 61.

11. For a slightly different but helpful historical overview, see Conyers, 68–69.

CHAPTER 5

1. For an excellent introduction to the history of the English Bible, see F. F. Bruce, *The History of the Bible in English*, 3d ed. (New York: Oxford University Press, 1988). For shorter introductions, see "Bible" by J. Orr, in *International Standard Bible Encyclopedia*, gen. ed. Geoffrey W. Bromiley, rev. ed. (Grand Rapids, Mich.: Eerdmans, 1979), 1:482–492; Allen Wikgren, "The English Bible," in *The Interpreter's Bible*, gen. ed. George Arthur Buttrick (New York: Abingdon Press, 1952), 1:84–105; and Neil R. Lightfoot, *How We Got the Bible* (Grand Rapids, Mich.: Baker Book House, 1963), 96–117.

2. Gordon D. Fee and Douglas Stuart, *How to Read the Bible for all Its Worth: A Guide to Understanding the Bible* (Grand Rapids, Mich.: Academie, Zondervan Publishing House, 1982), 34.

3. McKnight, *Opening the Bible*, 117.

4. *The Oxford Annotated Bible: Revised Standard Version*, ed. Herbert G. May and Bruce M. Metzger (New York: Oxford University Press, 1962), xiii.

5. R. C. Sproul, *Knowing Scripture* (Downers Grove, Ill.: InterVarsity Press, 1977), 118.

6. For the best recent introduction to translation theories, see Fee and Stewart, 35–36. This section is taken from their excellent analysis.

7. Updated from Fee and Stewart, 36. The abbreviations: KJV, King James Version; NKJV, New King James Version; NASB, New American Standard Bible; NRSV, New Revised Standard Version; NIV, New International Version; NAB, New American Bible (a Catholic version); GNB, Good News Bible; (also known as Today's English Version) JB, Jerusalem Bible; REB, Revised English Bible; CEB, Contemporary English Bible; Phillips, J. B. Phillips's translation; LB, Living Bible; CP, Cotton Patch Bible.

8. Fee and Stuart, 42.

9. From William Tyndale's preface to his New Testament of 1534; *Tyndale's New Testament*, ed. David Daniell (New Haven: Yale University Press, 1989), 15–16.

10. For a good introduction to this area, see James P. Martin, "Tools of the Interpreter," in Bernard L. Ramm et. al., *Hermeneutics* (Grand Rapids, Mich.: Baker Book House, 1987), 140–52.

11. Taken from Fee and Stuart, 220.

12. For more information, consult Tremper Longman, *Old Testament Commentary Survey* (Grand Rapids, Mich.: Baker Book House, 1991). This work is a buyer's guide to one-volume commentaries, sets, and individual commentaries.

13. Edgar V. McKnight, "Love," in *Holman Bible Dictionary*, gen. ed. Trent C. Butler (Nashville: Holman Bible Publishers, 1991), 896–8.

14. J. Orr, "Bible," in *The International Standard Bible Encyclopedia*, rev. ed., gen. ed. Geoffrey W. Bromiley (Grand Rapids, Mich.: Eerdmans, 1979), 1:482–92.

15. *The Table Talk of Martin Luther*, ed. with intro. by Thomas S. Kepler (New York: World Publishing Co., 1952), 22.

CHAPTER 6

1. The discussion which follows is an enlargement of the author's "Lecture Outlines for Biblical Hermeneutics" (Fort Worth, Tex.: Southwestern Baptist Theological Seminary, 1989), 5–27. Among the many good treatments of the history of biblical interpretation, the following books are especially helpful: John Rogerson, Christopher Rowland, and Barnabas Lindars, *The Study and Use of the Bible: The History of Christian Theology*, ed. Paul Avis, vol. 2 (Grand Rapids: Eerdmans, 1988); Robert M. Grant with David Tracy, *A Short History of the Interpretation of the Bible*, 2d ed. rev. (n.p.: Fortress Press, 1984 [1963]); A. Berkeley Mickelsen, *Interpreting the Bible* (Grand Rapids, Mich.: Eerdmans, 1963), 20–53; and Ramm, *Protestant Biblical Interpreta-* tion, 23–92. The classic text in the subject remains Frederic W. Farrar, *History of Interpretation* (Grand Rapids, Mich.: Baker, 1961). For excellent articles, see: John P. Newport, "Representative Historical and Contemporary Approaches to Biblical Interpretation, *"Faith and Mission III"*, 2 (Spring 1986), 32–48; and Robert M. Grant, John T. McNeill, and Samuel Terrien, "History of the Interpretation of the Bible," *The Interpreter's Bible* (New York: Abingdon, 1952), 1:106–41.

2. *The Babylonian Talmud*, Seder Mo'ed, Shabbath I, trans. I. Epstein (London: Sancino Press, 1938), 31a (I:140).

3. Farrar, 140–41.

4. *The First Epistle of Clement*, 12, *Ante-Nicene Fathers*, I:8.

5. *The Epistle of Barnabas*, x, Ante-Nicene Fathers, I:143.

6. Justin, *Dialogue with Trypho* 42, *Ante-Nicene Fathers*, 1:215–16.

7. Clement of Alexandria, *The Instructor* II:IV (*Ante-Nicene Fathers*, 2:248).

8. Stephen L. Wailes, *Medieval Allegories of Jesus' Parables* (Berkeley, Calif.: University of California Press, 1987), 138.

9. *Origen's Commentary on John, Ante-Nicene Fathers*, 10:396–99.

10. See Farrar, 213–19.

11. Augustine, Sermon 81, *Sermons on New Testament Lessons, Nicene and Post-Nicene Fathers*, first series, 6:503.

12. Augustine, *On the Psalms*, Nicene and Post-Nicene Fathers, first series, 8:515–16.

13. For more on the following, see Grant, 83–91.

14. Thomas, *Summa Theologica*, 1.Q1.8.

15. *Summa*, 1.Q1.10.

16. The outstanding treatment of contemporary interpretive theory is Anthony C. Thiselton, *New Horizons in Hermeneutics: The Theory* and *Practice of Transforming Biblical Reading* (Grand Rapids, Mich.: Zondervan, 1992).

17. Rudolf Bultmann, *History of the Synoptic Tradition*, rev. ed., trans. John Marsh (New York: Harper and Row, 1968), 284–91.

CHAPTER 7

1. The literature on the subject of Bible study methods is massive. In fact, today we smile at H. Wheeler Robinson's statement, made in 1943, that hermeneutics is "a rather neglected branch of Biblical study at the present time" ("The Higher Exegesis," *Journal* of Theological Studies 44 [1943], 143). The classic introductions to hermeneutical method remain Mickelsen, *Interpreting the Bible*; and Ramm, *Protestant Biblical Interpretation*. Other good sources are Dunnett, *The Interpretation of Holy Scripture*, Virkler, *Hermeneutics*; Fee and Stewart, 22–27; and Walter Henrichsen and Gayle Jackson, *Studying, Interpreting and Applying the Bible* (Grand Rapids: Lamplighter Books, Zondervan, 1990).

2. John Piper, *The Supremacy of God in Preaching* (Grand Rapids: Baker Book House, 1990), 42.

3. Fritz Rienecker, *A Linguistic Key to the Greek New Testament*, trans. and rev. Cleon L. Rogers, Jr. (Grand Rapids: Zondervan, 1980), 2:281.

4. Martin Luther, *Table Talk* 2:244–45; quoted in Conyers, 58.

5. For more on the literature of the Bible, see Leland Ryken, *How to Read the Bible as Literature* (Grand Rapids: Academie Books, Zondervan, 1984).

6. See James Montgomery Boice, *The Sermon on the Mount* (Grand Rapids, Mich.: Zondervan, 1972), 16–17.

7. This phrase as applied here is taken from Dunnett, 100.

8. Dwight L. Moody, *Secret Power* (Ventura, Calif.: Regal Books, 1987 [originally published by Fleming H. Revell, 1881], 80–81.

9. Ramm, 186; emphases his.

10. Quoted in *Parables, Etc.*, May, 1990, 8. For further reading here, see Conyers, 129–39.

11. For further reading here, see Conyers, 129–39.

12. In *Leaves of Gold*, ed. Clyde Francis Lytle, rev. ed. (Williamsport, Penn.: Coslett Publishing Company, 1948), 47.

CONCLUSION

1. Quoted in *The Christian Century*, 24 October 1990, 957.

2. Quoted in *Parables, Etc.*, April 1993, 5.

3. This schedule is taken from Robert H. Mounce, *Answers to Questions About the Bible* (Grand Rapids, Mich.: Baker Book House, 1979), 21–22.

4. Quoted in *Christian History*, vol. X, no. 1, 12.

5. Cited in *Preaching*, January-February 1993, 77.

6. Quoted in *The Pastor's Story File*, July 1992, 5.

7. Quoted in *Christianity Today*, 8 March 1993, 45.